Marvelous Minilessons
for Teaching
Intermediate Writing, Grades 4-6

Lori Jamison Rog

INTERNATIONAL
Reading Association

800 BARKSDALE ROAD, PO BOX 8139
NEWARK, DE 19714-8139, USA
www.reading.org

The International Reading Association attempts, through its publications, to provide a forum for a wide spectrum of opinions on reading. This policy permits divergent viewpoints without implying the endorsement of the Association.

Executive Editor, Books   Corinne M. Mooney
Editorial Production Manager   Shannon T. Fortner
Design and Composition Manager   Anette Schuetz

Project Editors   Stacey L. Reid and Susanne Viscarra

Cover   Design, Linda Steere; Photograph, Shutterstock

The publisher would appreciate notification where errors occur so that they may be corrected in subsequent printings and/or editions.

Library of Congress Cataloging-in-Publication Data

Rog, Lori Jamison.
    Marvelous minilessons for teaching intermediate writing, grades 4–6 / Lori Jamison Rog.
        p. cm.
    Includes bibliographical references and index.
    ISBN 978-0-87207-832-1 (alk. paper)
    1. English language—Composition and exercises—Study and teaching (Elementary) 2. English language—Composition and exercises—Study and teaching (Middle school) I. Title.
    LB1576.R645 2010
    372.62'3—dc22

                                2010041396

Suggested APA Reference
Rog, L.J. (2011). *Marvelous minilessons for teaching intermediate writing, grades 4–6*. Newark, DE: International Reading Association.

CONTENTS

 ori Jamison Rog is a teacher, consultant, and staff developer. She is the author of many articles and teacher's guides as well as seven books for teachers, including *Marvelous Minilessons for Teaching Beginning Writing, K–3*.

Lori has served as the K–12 literacy consultant for Regina Public Schools in Saskatchewan, Canada, as well as a reading assessment specialist with the Saskatchewan Department of Education, but the highlights of her professional career were her years as a classroom teacher for primary and intermediate grades.

Lori is an honorary lifetime member of the Saskatchewan Reading Council and a former member of the International Reading Association's Board of Directors.

She lives in an 1889 Victorian townhouse in downtown Toronto with her husband, Paul Kropp, who writes novels for young adults.

Currently, Lori is a private educational consultant who writes professional materials for teachers and consults with school districts. She has presented at many literacy conferences, from Nova Scotia to New Zealand and San Francisco to Dublin.

Author Information for Correspondence and Workshops
Please feel free to contact Lori with inquiries about this book or about consulting or professional development. She can be reached by e-mail at ljamison@sasktel.net, and her website is www.lorijamison.com.

Not long ago, I was working with a group of grades 4–6 teachers on the south side of Chicago. "We've got resources to the rafters for the K–3 classes, and money is starting to pour in for adolescent literacy," they said, "But we seem to be the forgotten group. Nobody's paying any attention to teaching the kids in the middle." There was some truth to what these teachers were saying. The research specifically related to preadolescents is skimpy. No grand federal programs have been directed their way. Even the nickname given to this age group—the tweens—suggests that they are defined by being in between—no longer children but not yet teenagers.

Yet, the tween group has its own unique characteristics. This preadolescent period is a time of significant cognitive and physical development. Students of this age are developing the language and thought processes to solve problems, to appreciate subtlety and humor, to apply logical rules and reasoning, and to appreciate differing opinions and points of view (Ontario Ministry of Education, 2008).

No longer are parents and teachers the primary influences; now adults must compete with peers and popular culture. Role models like children's cartoon and book characters have been supplanted by teen pop music and television celebrities. These tweens are also smarter about themselves, the world around them, and the adults with whom they interact.

We also see more gender differences in their tastes, activities, and habits than in younger grades. Gender differences have a huge impact on academic behavior and performance. In fact, according to Myra Barrs and Sue Pidgeon (1994), gender is the single biggest factor in determining what students read at this age. Elaine Millard (1997), one of the pioneers of research on boys and literacy, reports that there are significant gender differences when it comes to writing: At this age, girls write more easily, more prolifically, and more effectively than boys.

Why is writing important for our tweens? Writing is a survival tool that helps students organize their thoughts, solve problems, distinguish key ideas from supporting details, reflect on different perspectives, remember important ideas, and in general, develop the ability to communicate their ideas to others. Writing is critically important for school success, but it's also increasingly important in the wider world. Thomas Newkirk (2009) cites the increasing prevalence of new technologies that encourage writing for an audience— social networking sites such as Facebook and Twitter, blogs, comments on other people's blogs, websites, and user reviews of books, movies and music—as evidence that writing is an essential skill for citizens of the world.

Only a decade into the 21st century, we have seen tremendous changes in the impact of technology on writing. The National Council of Teachers of English's document *Writing in the 21st Century* (Yancey, 2009) states,

> This 21st century writing marks the beginning of a new era in literacy, a period we might call the Age of Composition, a period where composers become composers not through direct and formal instruction alone (if at all), but rather through what we might call an extracurricular social co-apprenticeship. (p. 5)

Today, 95% of fourth graders in the United States have access to computers in school, with a national average of one computer for every four students (Bausell, 2008). Word-processing programs allow students to write longer papers, make revisions and edits more easily, and produce printed work that looks practically professional (MacArthur, 1996). The *Writing Next* report (Graham & Perin, 2007) finds word processing to be an instructional innovation that has had a significant impact on the quality of student writing, especially for low-achieving writers.

Yet, the impact of technology is much more than simply word processing. Technology has changed not just the way we do writing but also the way we use it. In some cases, writing has become as much visual as verbal. Some argue that the page as the dominant form of communication is giving way to the computer screen (Snyder, 1998). Gunther Kress (2003), who coined the term *multimodal text*, emphasizes that we need to think of student writers not just as producers of print but also as designers and composers who are able to use a variety of media to construct and communicate information.

For young people, literacy is no longer just the private world of a reader and a book; it has become a social world of e-mail, text messaging, blogging, and tweeting. When e-mail first emerged, teachers saw it as a great opportunity to motivate student writers. However, this new genre did not follow a standard writing process, was done "on the fly," and had a standard of grammar and conventions that made teachers squirm. In fact, new modes of communication have spawned a whole new set of conventions in spelling, punctuation, and capitalization. Text such as "4getn u is hard 2 do, 4gtn me is up2 u, 4gt me not, 4gt me neva, but don't 4get, we're gr8 2gether" can be enough to make an English teacher's head spin (especially those of us for whom typing "great" is much more efficient than searching for *8* on the numerical row of the keyboard), but it remains a valid form of communication for a generation that may very well write more than any other in history.

The challenge for us as teachers is to help students understand the various forms and purposes of writing, so they know when emoticons and text messaging abbreviations are acceptable and when standard spelling and conventions are required. Technology has revolutionized the place of writing in the social and academic worlds and will continue to expand communication in ways not even imagined today. With good teaching, all of our students can be part of the writing revolution.

For too long, writing has been an incidental subject in school, the "neglected 'R,'" according to the National Commission on Writing in America's Schools and Colleges (2003). We're having students do an increasing amount of "writing to learn"—responses to reading, science logs, mathematics journals, and research reports—but not enough "learning to write." If we want our students to be better writers, we need to teach them what good writers do. We need to give them plenty of opportunities to practice. And, we need to allow them to experience the impact of their words in print for real audiences and real purposes.

An Overview of This Book

This book is about the explicit teaching of writing to the unique needs of students in the intermediate grades (4–6). It consists of 40 minilessons on a range of strategies and writers' techniques, from prewriting and planning to idea development and wordsmithing. Over 20 years ago, Lucy Calkins (1986) coined the term *minilesson* to describe brief, explicit instructional sessions that focus on a specific learning objective and provide opportunity for direct transfer to the student's own writing. I believe that the 10-minute minilesson is probably the greatest tool we have for teaching the habits of highly effective writers. I confess, however, that some of the lessons in this book have been known to stretch beyond the mini to the maxi in order to include both explicit instruction and guided practice. We need to remember that the bulk of writing workshop time should be devoted to student writing, and if the teaching piece goes on beyond 10 minutes or so, it may sometimes be necessary to stop the lesson and continue it the next day.

These are some of my favorite minilessons from my years of experience with young writers and my observations of good teaching in exemplary classrooms across the United States and Canada. The "teacher talk" scripts in the minilessons reflect the language I use when presenting these lessons to intermediate-grade writers. I frequently suggest that students turn and talk to a partner, as that dialogue helps them sort their ideas and stretch their thinking. The examples are actual samples of modeled writing, and vignettes are based on observations from actual classrooms (but all student and teacher names are pseudonyms). All of the minilessons are grounded in research and best practices in literacy instruction and designed to help our students gain proficiency and independence as writers. Like its companion volume, *Marvelous Minilessons for Teaching Beginning Writing, K–3* (Rog, 2007), this book offers novices and veterans alike a collection of practical, teacher-tested, and pupil-proven lesson ideas to add to their teaching toolboxes.

When teaching the intermediate grades, it is all too easy to focus on the mechanics of writing: punctuation, capitalization, spelling, and grammar. Although conventional spelling and grammar are critical to written communication, there is much more to good writing. I have chosen in this book to focus on the craft of writing rather than the conventions. However, we know that instruction in conventions is most effective (perhaps *only* effective) in the context of writing (Graham & Perin, 2007), and several of the lessons in this book incorporate grammatical elements into the writer's craft. For example, the minilesson on dialogue includes instruction in the use of quotation marks (see Dabble in Dialogue in Chapter 4); the minilesson on sentence flipping for fluency integrates the teaching of sentence structure and prepositional phrases (see Flip the Sentence in Chapter 7); a minilesson on vivid word choice incorporates the study of parts of speech (see Vivid Verbs Bring Writing to Life in Chapter 7).

Decisions about how to structure this book have come from my ongoing work with teachers and students. Over the years, key issues continue to emerge over and over: How can I help kids get started? How do I teach students to move past lists of details to elaborate on the most important ideas? What techniques can my students learn to help them craft their writing more eloquently? Even those literacy teachers who are quite comfortable teaching narrative writing often seek assistance with other nonfiction genres, such as persuasive and informational texts. Of course, there is also always the burning issue, How can I help students demonstrate what they know and can do on large-scale writing assessments? Answers to all of these questions can be found in the chapters of this book.

Chapter 1, "The Writing Workshop: A Predictable Structure," provides an overview of the writing workshop and offers suggestions for organizing and managing the writing program at the intermediate level, planning effective minilessons and conferences, and guiding students on the journey to publication as we help them develop increasing independence as writers.

Chapter 2, "Unit Planning and the Six-Traits Framework," addresses the important link between planning and assessment. This chapter includes a unit planning template that integrates genre-based instruction and the powerful six-traits framework (Culham, 2003; Spandel, 2001).

Getting started with writing can be a monumental challenge for writers of all ages and stages. **Chapter 3, "The Power of Prewriting,"** offers a range of prewriting tools and strategies to help get developing writers over that initial hurdle, from graphic organizers to pretelling and mind-mapping.

Minilessons on idea development are offered in **Chapter 4, "Elaboration: Adding Details to Details."** How often have we teachers agonized over the "breakfast to bed" story—a string of ideas without elaboration, each receiving the same amount of attention and emphasis? Knowing how and when to elaborate can take a piece of laundry-list writing to a well-rounded narrative.

The next two chapters focus on genres that are ubiquitous in intermediate curricula. **Chapter 5, "Researching and Writing Informational Texts,"** provides a sequential process for taking a piece of research writing from gathering notes to drafting paragraphs to revising for word and sentence variety. **Chapter 6, "Writing to Persuade,"** follows a similar process as it guides students in planning, drafting, revising a piece of persuasive writing— with lessons on support for opinions, facts and statistics, and anticipating the argument.

Chapter 7, "The Writer's Craft: Writing With Rhythm and Flair," offers minilessons that are not so much about *what* the writing says but *how* it is expressed. Writers' techniques, such as using similes, vivid verbs, and well-crafted sentences, are included in this chapter.

Chapter 8, "Success on the Test," focuses on that most unique of nonlife skills we must teach in school: scoring well on a writing assessment. While emphasizing that the best test preparation is a strong writing program, this chapter offers five minilessons on strategies for success on tests and beyond, including summarizing, responding to literature, and budgeting time effectively.

Finally, **Chapter 9, "Supporting Struggling Writers and Beating the Odds,"** touches on ideas for reaching the most challenging of students—the struggling writer—and closes with some interesting research that offers hope for beating the odds in high-poverty schools.

What Makes This Book Unique?

Several textual elements have been designed to be practical and useful for teachers:

- Each chapter begins with an overview of why the topic matters to intermediate students, a review of the research, an introduction to the minilessons, and additional ideas for instruction and reflection.

- Each minilesson focuses on a specific learning goal, a reminder that writing instruction is less about the task itself and more about what the student is learning as a writer. Identifying the learning goal, standard, or proficiency up front makes instruction more relevant and assessment more straightforward.

- Each minilesson is linked to one or more of the six traits of effective writing.

- Each minilesson has four main components: Introduction, Instruction, Guided Practice, and Independent Application. The Introduction states the learning goal and links it to students' prior knowledge. The Instruction section offers explicit teaching and modeling of the strategy. Guided Practice enables students to try out the strategy in a safe, supported, and success-oriented setting, often in pairs or small groups. Finally, through the Independent Application, there is always the invitation and expectation that students will apply the strategy to their own writing.

- Teacher supports in the minilessons include sample writing pieces to use as models and graphic organizers to support guided practice. In addition, italicized "teacher talk" in each lesson serves as a model for the language I might use in presenting the minilesson to students. Of course, this is just a guide, and teachers will want to modify this script to suit their students and individual teaching styles.

- Space for marginal notes encourages teachers to reflect on their instruction and make observations about how they might change or adapt a lesson in future. The note-taking area in the margins may also support questions or comments for book study groups or professional learning communities.

I hope there will be many different audiences for this book. The beginning or preservice teacher will find dozens of tried-and-true minilessons for teaching writing. The experienced writing teacher may find some new twists on familiar ideas. The coach, literacy leader, or consultant will have a package of materials to use for demonstration lessons or to put into teachers' hands. This book is not intended to be a program or prescription but rather a menu of ideas from which teachers may draw to complement and supplement their writing programs. Throughout the book, I use the words *we* and *our* as a reminder that the quest for excellence in teaching and learning is a collaborative effort. I am proud to say that I am a teacher and a lifelong learner. I invite the readers of this book to learn along with me.

CHAPTER 1

The Writing Workshop: A Predictable Structure

Walk into Ms. Lindsay's fifth-grade writing class, and you're likely to see children all over the room, engaged in a range of different activities. José and Hayden have their heads bent over José's paper, engrossed in a peer conference. Charlotte is working at a "private office," a desk with a cardboard carrel. Amir is at the bookshelf starting research on his report on Pluto. Yung has a colored pen in one hand and the dictionary in the other; she's editing her own writing before submitting it for publication. This is what writing workshop looks like in Ms. Lindsay's—and countless other—classrooms. Like "real writers," these students are writing, consulting, researching, changing, talking, reading, and generally making decisions about their own work.

Writers follow a variety of routines that generally involve planning and preparation, getting ideas down on paper, rewriting, polishing, rewriting some more, and finally making the work public. In school, we have come to call these routines "the writing process," as defined by Donald Graves in 1983. Although this process may vary from writer to writer and from task to task, it usually consists of a series

The Writing Process
• Getting started
• Getting it down
• Getting it good
• Getting it right
• Getting it out

of activities that includes prewriting (planning, generating, and organizing ideas), drafting, revising (making changes to improve clarity and style), editing (fixing mechanical errors), and publishing (sharing with an audience). I like to tell intermediate students that the writing process is all about getting started, getting it down on paper, getting it good, getting it right, and getting it out to a reader.

Of course, not every writer or piece of writing goes through the same sequence at the same pace and at the same time. Not every piece of writing is taken to publication. Some pieces of writing take forever to plan, while others are quickly drafted then revised over and over again. Some novelists tell us that they will revise a piece of work dozens of times. It is said that Thomas Jefferson made over 30 revisions to his original draft of the Declaration of Independence. Then, Congress made another 80 changes to it before it appeared in the form we now know. (An Internet search for "Declaration of Independence draft" will generate images of the actual document, full of strike-throughs, additions, and other revisions.)

The ebbs and flows of the writing process are challenging enough for an individual writer, so how do we manage this in a classroom full of writers? The writing workshop is an organizational structure that allows students to operate at different stages of the writing process at any given time. The great strength of the writing workshop is that it fosters student independence, freeing up the teacher to monitor, assess, and provide support that extends the reach of his or her young writers (Graves, 1983).

The Writing Workshop

Lucy Calkins (1983) has described the writing workshop as a deliberately predictable environment where the unpredictable can happen. In any writing workshop, from kindergarten to college, there are three basic time components: teaching time, writing time, and sharing time. The workshop typically starts with explicit instruction, usually in the form of a 5- to 10-minute minilesson (Atwell, 1998; Calkins, 1986). The largest portion of the writing workshop is dedicated to sustained writing and conferring with teacher and peers. As the students write, the teacher circulates among them to offer brief support and advice or to conduct individual conferences. The workshop generally ends with a brief opportunity for sharing and celebrating, often called the "author's chair" (Graves & Hansen, 1983).

Writing Workshop
- Teaching time: 10–15 min.
- Writing time: 25–35 min.
- Sharing time: 10 min.

How might this structure look in our intermediate classrooms? Given the importance of a predictable routine, explicit instruction, sustained writing time, and opportunities to confer and receive feedback, the writing workshop requires at least 45–60 minutes. The minimum 45 minutes, for example, might comprise a 10-minute minilesson, 25 minutes of writing, and a 10-minute sharing period.

Experts such as Graves advocate scheduling writing workshop every day. In our busy school timetables, how can we find 45–60 minutes a day for writing? Perhaps it might require some creative timetabling, such as splitting the 90-minute literacy block equally between reading and writing workshop, or offering reading and writing workshops on alternate days. Maybe there are existing practices we might change or reconsider to make time for writing. For example, many classrooms use precious writing time creating daily journals. Although this practice may have benefits in helping students organize their thoughts or share feelings, it rarely translates to better writing. That's because journals tend to be "hands off"; there is no explicit teaching of writing and no accountability on the part of the writers to demonstrate craft or process.

Another way to find time for writing is to reconsider dedicated grammar or language arts instruction. There is more than 75 years of research indicating that grammar instruction in isolation does not improve writing (Hillocks, 1986); in fact, the *Writing Next* analysis of research on adolescent writers found that grammar instruction in isolation was one of the few practices that actually had a negative correlation with improving writing (Graham & Perin, 2007). Embedding grammar instruction into the writing workshop makes better use of everyone's time, because it provides opportunities for immediate and authentic application and practice of grammatical concepts.

Teaching Time: The Power of the Minilesson

In the past, some of us have misinterpreted the writing workshop as an arrangement in which the teacher functioned as a "guide on the side," hoping that our students would flourish as writers simply by writing. While this approach may have produced *more* writing, it didn't always lead to *better* writing. If we want our students to become more proficient writers, we know that we must teach "with a capital *T*" (Atwell, 1998, p. 22). Students need organized, focused instruction on the skills, techniques, and strategies used by writers to take a piece of writing from conception to publication. The minilesson is one of the most powerful structures we have for providing that instruction.

Every writing workshop starts with teaching: explicit instruction in an element of the writing process, conventions, or craft. Because these teaching sessions are brief and focused, we call them minilessons (Calkins, 1986). We want the bulk of the writing workshop time to be for *student writing*; therefore, our minilessons shouldn't run more than 10–15 minutes. Most often, minilessons are presented to the whole class; however, at times, we may pull small groups of students with similar needs for a focused lesson.

The writing minilesson offers us the opportunity to teach a range of skills and strategies. We might introduce a new planning tool or revising technique. We might model an element of the writer's craft, such as showing rather than telling. We might even use the opportunity to establish workshop routines: how to organize a writing folder, how to conduct an effective peer conference, how to manage materials, or how to request a teacher conference. The writing minilesson is also the most appropriate place to teach writing conventions, like quotation marks, subject–verb agreement, or sentence structure.

The best way to teach children how to write is to show them what writers do. Our students need to see us write. We need to model writing and articulate the in-the-head thinking that goes on as writers make decisions about what to write and how to commit those ideas to paper. In an interview with *Instructor* magazine, Graves (n.d.) was asked, "If you had to choose one thing teachers should do when teaching writing, what would it be?" (para. 15). He replied,

> Write yourself. Invite children to do something you're already doing. If you're not doing it, Hey, the kids say, I can't wait to grow up and not have to write, like you…. You can't ask someone to sing a duet with you until you know the tune yourself. (para. 16)

There are several different levels of modeled writing, from "I do" through "we do" to "you do." The gradual release of responsibility model (Pearson & Gallagher, 1983) starts with explicit instruction, moves through guided support, and finally reaches independent application. Explicit instruction in writing often starts with *modeled writing,* in which the teacher demonstrates and thinks aloud as he or she writes. In a *shared writing* lesson, the teacher and students compose the text together while the teacher scribes. In *interactive writing*, the students and teacher compose collaboratively, and students take turns doing the writing. It's important for students to have opportunities for *guided practice*, with activities that scaffold and support them as they practice a new strategy or craft, before sending them off on their own for *independent application.* What distinguishes guided practice from merely assigning writing? For me, the difference is a focus on the strategy or learning goal rather than on the writing product.

Almost any kind of enlarged print works well for modeled writing. Some teachers like to use an overhead projector, because it enables them to face their students. Others prefer large flipcharts to keep the students physically close. Today's interactive whiteboards make modeling and demonstration easy and accessible. Regardless of the level of technology we employ, it's important to keep the modeled piece on hand to revisit in future lessons.

The minilessons in this book all follow the same structure:

- *Introduction* links the minilesson to prior learning and explicitly introduces the lesson goal.
- *Instruction* explains the strategy, usually through teacher modeling.
- *Guided Practice* offers the students an opportunity to try out the strategy with support.
- *Independent Application* asks students to try the strategy on their own.

With only about 10 minutes for explicit teaching in the writing workshop, we want to make sure that our minilesson packs a punch. Based on research from experts such as Calkins (2004), Graves (1983), and Patricia Cunningham and colleagues (Cunningham, Cunningham, Hall, & Moore, 2005), as well as experience from hundreds of classrooms, the following are some guidelines for effective preparation and delivery of minilessons.

1. *Use assessment to guide instruction.* There is no program that can tell us what to teach and when. No publisher knows what our students need at any given time. Only we can know that, and we get the information by constantly assessing our students' writing to determine what they can do well and what they need to know next.

2. *Keep it brief.* The operative term is *mini*; don't let the minilesson turn into a maxilesson. The primary purpose of the writing workshop is student writing! Avoid the temptation to extend the lesson portion at the expense of writing time. If necessary, spread the teaching over two days.

3. *Focus on only one key learning goal per lesson.* When we think aloud during the modeled writing lesson, it's very easy to run in a dozen different directions at once. It's important to be very clear about what we want students to learn from this lesson and focus on this learning with the students.

4. *Tell students what they will learn in the lesson.* Who has time to turn a minilesson into a guessing game? Not only should we be clear ourselves about the focus of the lesson, but we should also make sure that the students know what they will be learning. It helps to focus the learning when we start a lesson with a simple statement:

> *Boys and girls, today you are going to learn about revising to add details to a piece of writing.*

5. *Start by connecting to the known.* We all learn best when new information is linked to existing knowledge. Jean Piaget (1952) calls this existing knowledge "schema" and posits that learning involves *assimilating* new information into our schema or *accommodating* our schema to include the new information. When we open a minilesson with a connection to what students already know, we are preparing their schema to accept new learning. For example,

> *Boys and girls, you already know how to revise a piece of writing by inserting details. Today you're going to learn another revising technique: replacing words and details.*

6. *Be explicit and direct.* Not all of our teaching needs to be interactive. Sometimes we may want to involve the students in composing or brainstorming; at other times, we will deliver the information directly. We need to make the most of a very limited amount of time for a minilesson, which requires making choices about the most efficient way to achieve the learning goals.

7. *Expect students to be accountable for their learning.* Make it clear that you will be looking for some demonstration of the learning in the students' writing:

> *Today, when I come around to see your writing, I want you to show me a place where you added a showing detail to a telling statement.*

8. *Reteach as necessary.* We can't expect that our students will master a writing concept after one minilesson. Some kids will profess to have never heard of a concept that we taught just last week! Repeating a few lessons several times, with frequent opportunities for practice, will go further in helping our students master the habits of highly effective writers than touching on many concepts just once.

Writing Time

Writing time occupies the largest portion of the writing workshop. Most often, students will be working on self-selected writing during the workshop, although sometimes they will work on guided or assigned writing tasks. At some point in the workshop, they should be expected to try out what they learned in the day's minilesson. This expectation may entail revisiting a finished draft, integrating their learning into a work in progress, or starting a new piece of writing.

Of course, writing time is not exclusively about putting pen to paper. During this time, a student may write for a while, do some research, confer with a writing partner, or read a piece of writing aloud to himself or another student. Writing workshop packs a powerful pedagogical punch, because it immerses students in all of the language arts: reading, writing, listening, and speaking.

Writing is a social process for most writers (Roser & Bomer, 2005). Through conversations before, during, and after writing, students clarify their own thinking, rehearse, revise their writing, and collect ideas from others, including the teacher. At times, however, some writers prefer an environment without distractions, so I like to distinguish between "silent" writing time, when no talking or movement is permitted, and "quiet" writing time, when students are free to converse and confer in soft voices. Jennifer Jacobson (2010) advocates starting writing time with the "Quiet Ten"—10 minutes of silent thinking and writing time that is signaled by the sounds of soft music.

One of the greatest benefits of the writing workshop structure is the development of independent learning habits. An important lesson for students is, "you're never *done* with writing workshop." Students learn very quickly not to ask that dreaded question, "What do I do when I'm done?" because the answer is always, "When you're done, you've just begun!" When they've finished what they're working on, students have the option of starting a new piece of writing, finishing an incomplete draft, or revising a piece of writing. It is an important step in learning for writers to take responsibility for their own learning.

Writers basically need just two tools for writing workshop: something to write with and something to write on. For intermediate grades, I prefer to have students write on loose-leaf paper. Using only one side of the page, they write double-spaced, whether it's word-processed or written longhand, which enables them to do all revisions on the same sheet. I try to avoid having students recopy anything until the final draft; let's not make revision any more painful than it already is! Of course, that means we have to provide them with the tools and symbols for revision: carets for inserting words and short ideas, strike-throughs for deleting or replacing information, spider legs for drawing a line from a point in the text to information on another part of the page, paper stretchers for taping in an extra section of paper, and of course, cutting and pasting to reorganize information.

To keep the writing organized, I like to use a three-pocket writing folder, such as the one pictured in Figure 1.1. The first pocket holds ideas, plans, and topics for future writing. The second pocket holds works in progress and incomplete drafts. The third pocket holds finished drafts that have not yet been revised and edited for publication. These folders are simple to make from easily available materials, can be personalized by each student, and if laminated, are durable enough to carry over from one year to the next.

FIGURE 1.1. Three-Pocket Writing Folder Instructions

Materials: One 24″ × 36″ sheet of colored poster board, tag board, or Bristol board (as heavy in weight as possible while still folding effectively)

Directions:
1. Fold the bottom third of the paper up to form a pocket along the bottom.
2. Fold the entire page into three equal vertical sections.
3. Label the first pocket "Writing Ideas," the second pocket "Works in Progress," and the third "Finished Drafts."
4. Have the student personalize his or her own folder.
5. Laminate the folder, if possible.
6. Use a long-armed stapler to reinforce the three pockets.

Conferences: The Teacher's Role

During writing time, the teacher circulates among the students, offering support, gentle nudges, guiding questions, and explicit suggestions for improvement. Teacher conferences are one of the most powerful ways of differentiating writing instruction and improving writing proficiency, because they provide us with the opportunity to offer individualized instruction at the point of need (Calkins, 2004). Conferring facilitates the "just-in-time teaching" that helps our students grow as readers, writers, and thinkers. As Ralph Fletcher and JoAnn Portalupi (2001) tell us, conferences enable teachers to "stretch the writer" by teaching strategies intended to take the student beyond a piece of writing to improve "*all* the writing that student will do" (p. 52).

There are three main types of teacher conferences conducted in the writing workshop: quick "status-of-the-class" conferences to determine each student's plan for the day, "TAG" conferences for revision, and editing conferences for final polishing before publishing. In addition to teacher conferences, many teachers like to include student-to-student peer conferences.

Status-of-the-Class Conference

Before writing time begins, we want to get an overview of what each student will be working on that day. Students will be at different stages of the writing process at any given time; some may be starting to draft a new composition, and others may be in the final stages of publication. A daily status-of-the-class assessment requires students to articulate their plans for the day and gives the teacher a "lay of the land." There are different approaches to handling the status of the class. Many teachers call out students' names one by one to ask what they are working on or what stage of the process they are engaged in. Other teachers have a pocket chart or work board on which students post their plans for the day.

I prefer to have each student maintain an individual writing log (see the reproducible on the following page). At the beginning of writing workshop, the students take a few minutes to record the date and their plans for the day. They might write something like, "Edit my piece 'My Camping Trip,' find a topic for a new piece, and start planning." Then, at the end of writing workshop, we allocate a few minutes to record what was accomplished. For example, the same student might write, "'My Camping Trip' edited and in the teacher's editing conference box, started planner for piece on my papa." I find that this is a good way for students to take responsibility for planning their time, and it gives me another tool for assessing their writing process. As the students are beginning to work, I can do a quick walkabout to check writing logs, ask questions, and make sure that everyone is ready to write.

Writing Log

Date	What I Plan to Work on Today	What I Got Done Today

TAG Conference

The heart of the writing workshop is the TAG conference (Rog, 1996; Rog & Kropp, 2004), which is a process for conferring with students in order to improve the clarity and effectiveness of a piece of writing. *TAG* is an acronym: Tell something you like, ask questions, and give advice.

This writing conference guides student revision and offers a powerful opportunity for brief, focused, individual teaching at the point of student need. The TAG conference starts with specific and focused praise for the strengths of the piece. This important step affirms what the writer has accomplished and makes him or her more receptive to hearing constructive questions and advice. Asking questions about the writing empowers the writer and reminds him or her that there is a reader on the other end of the writing. Asking questions does not imply a criticism of the writing but simply suggests that there may be some ideas that might be expressed more clearly and effectively for a reader. The challenge in this process is to ask meaningful questions that will lead to a piece of writing that is more interesting, clear, and powerful. Questions usually focus on either the content of the text or decisions made by the writer, for example,

TAG Conference
• Tell something you like.
• Ask questions.
• Give advice.

- *What do you mean by...?*
- *Why did you decide to insert this detail right here?*

The final step of the TAG conference is to give advice—suggestions intended to improve the quality of the writing as well as give the writer some strategies to use down the road. Sometimes the advice will address clarification of content:

I think you should add in the part that explains how your dog got out of the yard.

At other times, the suggestion may apply a writing strategy:

Why don't you add a little dialogue here to make the character's voice come through?

Note that we should not supply the actual wording, but we want to give students a tool or strategy to make the piece better.

The words *suggestion* and *advice* are perhaps a tad euphemistic, as these offerings are not optional. If the students are to become better writers, they need to practice the strategies and techniques that good writers use. Research tells us that when students have opportunities to revise their writing based on specific and focused feedback, the quality of their writing improves significantly (Hillocks, 1986). That's why I'm careful not to overwhelm students with too many changes—no more than two or three suggestions at most.

We're not going to turn a piece of fifth-grade writing into a Pulitzer Prize–winning essay; our job is to turn that fifth grader into a *better* writer.

Too often, our students are resistant to revision. They know the message they intended to convey, and if they had a better idea, they'd have written it the first time around! Even if they don't see their writing as the embodiment of perfection, they often just don't know what to do to make the writing better. The TAG conference helps writers see their work from a reader's point of view. What's missing? What's unclear? What's irrelevant or unnecessary? The TAG conference can provide that just-in-time teaching to improve not only today's piece of writing but also strategies for future writing. It's been my experience that when the students know specifically what they are to do (and know they don't have to rewrite the entire piece), even the most reluctant writer will go back and make the necessary revisions. Most writers, even intermediate students, really do want their writing to be clear and well crafted. What a switch from the old attitude of "it's perfect just the way it is!"

An effective TAG conference requires preparation and thoughtfulness on the part of the teacher. When a student places a piece of writing into my TAG basket, my homework is to read it and plan the comments I will make. I need to be able to see as many students as possible during writing time, and I simply can't read a piece and offer meaningful comments on the spot. My goal is to conduct the legendary "three-minute conference" proposed by Graves (1983) in his pioneering work on writing process so that I can spread my time and attention around evenly.

In my writing workshop, students *must* have a TAG conference on every piece of writing they choose to publish. Although it would be nice to confer with them on every piece they write, given the restraints of time and class size, that's pretty difficult. For the most part, I only confer with students on pieces that they are taking to publication.

Top Tips for TAG Conferences
1. *Be specific.* Comments like "nice work" and "needs work" do nothing to help either the writer or the writing.
2. *Focus on content and clarity, not conventions.* This is not the time to remind students about spelling or punctuation.
3. *Be brief.* Focus on only two or three things at most. Keep the information manageable for the students and the time manageable for you.
4. *Plan ahead.* Read the piece and plan the TAG conference ahead of time to make the most of teacher time and talent.
5. *Make students accountable.* You're doing your part to help students become better writers; they have to do their part to complete the revisions.

Editing Conference

The final type of conference is the polish-to-publish conference, otherwise known as the editing conference, which takes place only after all revisions are completed and the writer is ready to fix up spelling, punctuation, and grammar. We correct mechanical errors to make the writing accessible to a reader. That's why we don't spend a lot of time correcting until just before publication.

Some teachers believe that they must be the final editor for published work, just as professional writers have copyeditors who proofread their work.

But we're teachers, not editors. An editor's job is to produce a clean piece of writing; the teacher's job is to produce more skillful writers.

For me, the degree of editing support that I give students depends on how public the writing will be. When writing is going out into the world, I usually do a final edit of the piece to fix all errors. I don't want outside readers to be distracted from my students' content and craft by missing punctuation or misspelled words. But for classroom publication, I prefer to use the editing conference to focus on a few key teaching points that I feel are developmentally appropriate for that student, such as a spelling pattern, a run-on sentence, or a misplaced apostrophe. This is also a good opportunity to reinforce the differences between standard spelling and chat acronyms—and when each is appropriate.

It is always a balancing act between setting standards for correctness and encouraging students to take risks with language and structure. The more risks students take in sentence structure and vocabulary, the more errors they are likely to make. Ultimately, I want intermediate students to take responsibility for their own editing rather than rely on a teacher. Sometimes that means work will be published with mechanical errors in it. Research shows that when students attend to their own errors, they are more likely to learn from them (Hansen, 1987). Experts such as Calkins (1986) and Cunningham et al. (2005) caution us that when teachers conduct the final edit of a piece of writing, they are taking the "ownership" of the writing away from the writer. As always, it is a call that depends largely on the situation and the individual student.

> ## A Simple Editing Technique
>
> Read the piece sentence by sentence, reading every sentence twice.
>
> - During the first reading, listen for overall meaning and syntax. Fix grammar and punctuation.
> - During the second reading, read word by word, tapping under each word as you read, to find spelling errors.

A simple editing routine I suggest is to provide a collection of brightly colored skinny markers for editing. As students read their work sentence by sentence, they tap under each word, leaving a dot. This helps them focus on the individual words rather than the overall meaning. If they notice errors, they either strike through the word and correct it on the spot or circle the word and look it up in the dictionary later.

Peer Conference

In addition to teacher conferences, student-to-student peer conferences can also provide valuable learning for both the writer and the partner or partners. Peter Elbow (1973) popularized the idea of peer conferences in his book *Writing Without Teachers*. Anne Ruggles Gere (1987) concurs that peer conferences are particularly effective in supporting audience awareness. However, Betty Bamberg (2003) points out that students need instruction and practice in how to effectively function in peer groups. In fact, in later writing,

Elbow revised some of his earlier thinking to make the peer conference more structured and directed (Elbow & Belanoff, 2000).

The "stars and wishes" peer conference, described in the minilesson **Tell Me More: Powerful Peer Conferences** (see Chapter 4), is an adaptation of the TAG conference. Students confer with each other to offer compliments (stars) and questions (wishes) about a piece of writing. Of course, it's as vital to explicitly teach the peer conference as it is with any other writing skill or strategy. Taking time to model the conference structure, then providing students with opportunities for guided practice, will have lasting benefits for effective peer conferences.

Students need language to talk to one another about the content and craft of writing. Otherwise, they fall into the trap of pointing out misplaced punctuation or slips in spelling. Although this type of peer editing may (or may not) reduce some of the teacher's editing burden, it really doesn't teach either student participating in the conference much about being a better writer. I encourage students to sit facing one another, with the writer reading his or her piece aloud, so there is less temptation for the partner to focus on errors in conventions.

That's where rubrics, such as the six-traits framework described in Chapter 2, come in. These assessment tools guide readers in looking at all the elements of writing— ideas, organization, voice, word choice, sentence fluency, and conventions—and help them understand the criteria that make writing effective. The six traits also build a common language for teachers and students to talk to one another about writing.

Effective Peer Conferences
• Stars: What I like about the piece.
• Wishes: Questions about content or craft.

When students are taught to have meaningful conferences with peers, they learn to be more critical readers of both their peers' and their own writing. George Hillocks (1986) describes a study in which sixth-grade students in inner-city schools were taught to evaluate writing using defined criteria. Not only did the students become adept at assessing the writing of others, but also they were able "to internalize criteria which then served as guides for their own independent writing" (p. 158).

Sharing Time

Ending the writing workshop with sharing time brings closure to the session with an opportunity to reflect and celebrate writing (Graves & Hansen, 1983). Some teachers designate a special "author's chair" just for this purpose. For intermediate students, I find a music stand works very well as a podium, and if we can add a microphone, it's even better. Everyone must take a turn at sharing; it is an expectation of our writing community. As long as students know when their turn is coming, they can prepare themselves by choosing a piece of writing and practicing it for fluency and expression. I usually allow students to read any piece of writing that they haven't shared before, whether it's published or in process.

It's important to teach the audience how to respond appropriately in sharing time. Even in intermediate grades, we often have to model and practice good listening behaviors. Sharing time is a wonderful opportunity to build the language and habits of stars and wishes, setting the stage for effective peer conferences (see page 59).

The Publication Journey

Cunningham and her colleagues (Cunningham et al., 2005) recommend that students publish one out of every three pieces they draft. This teaches them to be selective about what they publish and ensures that there will always be something in the writing folder to use for guided practice or strategy work. Figure 1.2 illustrates the publication journey.

When students have three pieces in the finished drafts section of their writing folders, they select one to take to publication. They place the selected piece in the teacher's TAG basket and wait to be called for a TAG conference. In the meantime, they may start a new cycle of planning and drafting. Some teachers require students to have a peer conference before the teacher conference.

FIGURE 1.2. The Publication Journey

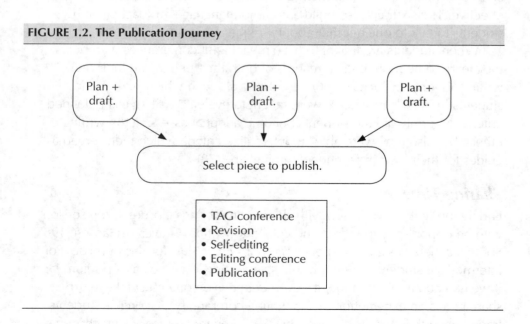

Plan + draft.   Plan + draft.   Plan + draft.

Select piece to publish.

- TAG conference
- Revision
- Self-editing
- Editing conference
- Publication

Following the TAG conference, the student completes the required revisions, performs a self-edit for conventions, then places the piece in the teacher's editing basket for a polish-to-publish conference. The final step is publication—by rewriting, word processing, illustrating, binding, or whatever process is used in the classroom. I sometimes ask parent volunteers to do the final word processing if students' access to computers or their keyboarding skills are limited.

Making the Most of Technology

Many teachers have students word-process their published writing. Word processing makes the published piece look more professional and facilitates last-minute revision and editing, but computers can be much more than glorified typewriters in our intermediate writing classrooms. What can we do to provide a full range of writing experiences that take advantage of what technology has to offer while balancing social networking communication and formal writing conventions?

1. *Familiarize students with keyboarding as early as possible.* This doesn't necessarily mean traditional touch typing but rather helping kids develop a system of automaticity with the keyboard. As long as students need to hunt and peck for every letter, it will interfere with their thinking processes as they write. The whole point of keyboarding is to allow the writer's fingers to move as quickly as his or her brain. When keyboarding becomes automatic, students can plan and draft as well as publish their writing on the computer.

2. *Require students to print a copy of each draft.* It's too easy for intermediate students to mislay files, lose revisions, or fail to make changes at all. For instructional purposes, you need to see evidence of revision and proof of process, and whether we like it or not, the hard copy is the most reliable.

3. *Teach the proper places for symbols and for standard spelling and mechanics.* There is no point in railing against emoticons and text-messaging abbreviations; instead, teach students when these typographic symbols are appropriate and when they're not. While texting to friends who understand their symbols can be perfectly appropriate, these acronyms probably won't make Grandma ROFL.

4. *Encourage the publication of multimodal texts.* Not every type of writing requires a paper report with indented paragraphs and a title centered at the top. Could a PowerPoint presentation or a wiki be equally useful? Encourage students to blend print and pictures, and teach them how to lay out a page efficiently, so the urge for graphic design doesn't overwhelm the need to craft the text.

5. *Combat the cut-and-paste culture generated by Internet research.* Require students to use a variety of print and Web-based sources to gather information. Teach students how to be critical readers and to discern factual information from opinions and inconsistencies. Explain the difference between effective use of quotations, how to cite references, and the pitfalls of plagiarism. (See Chapter 5, "Researching and Writing Informational Texts," for ideas.)

It's easy to create books of published writing by binding pages together with plastic coils. Each time a new piece is published, simply open the coils and insert the new piece. This makes a wonderful collection of the student's writing and an interesting portfolio of his or her progress as a writer over the course of the year.

After Publication

For most students, it takes three to four weeks to make the publication journey, depending on the frequency and length of the writing workshop. This highly predictable structure keeps the writing workshop manageable for teachers and students, and students only have to keep track of three pieces of writing at a time. We can allocate time for conferences and instruction more evenly and adjust the publication cycle for differing student needs and abilities.

As students complete each writing cycle, I have them submit their published copy and all three rough drafts. When I evaluate their writing, I'll look at different pieces of writing for different things. Perhaps I've had them practice a strategy on a draft in progress, or perhaps I'm looking for automatic spelling (as opposed to editing) of high-frequency words. The drafts can sometimes provide more—or different—insight into the student's writing process than the "clean" copy. In Chapter 2, we'll examine the trials and tribulations of assessment and how it fits into the planning process.

CHAPTER 2

Unit Planning and the Six-Traits Framework

"How do you evaluate writing workshop?" If I had a dollar for every time I was asked this question, I'd be wealthy today! The thing is, we don't actually evaluate writing workshop. Instead, we evaluate the students' progress toward the goals that have been set for them. Therefore, in writing workshop—as in any evaluation—we need to begin with the end in mind. What do we want our students to know and be able to do as a result of this teaching? Answering this essential question should be the first step in any instructional planning.

As teachers, we plan all the time. We make lesson plans, day plans, unit plans, and yearly plans. But whether we're designing a 10-minute minilesson or an extended unit of study, there are certain common considerations. Over 60 years ago, Ralph Tyler (1949/1969) introduced a four-step model of curriculum planning that started with articulating the educational purposes the instruction is intended to serve, then creating learning activities and assessment tools to achieve those purposes. Although the Tyler rationale still influences academic thinking today, classroom teachers do not always plan this way (Yinger, 1980).

In practice, teachers are more inclined to start with activities, topics, textbooks, or favorite lessons, which is why Grant Wiggins and Jay McTighe (1998) call their approach to curriculum planning "backward design." It asks teachers to shift their thinking from activities to goals as they design curricular units. Wiggins and McTighe advocate starting with the end—the desired results, standards, and goals—then designing the curriculum around supporting learners in achieving those goals. As James Stronge (2007) asserts in his work on qualities of effective teachers, instructional planning that clearly identifies learning objectives and links learning activities to those objectives is essential for effective teaching.

How do we determine goals for learning? Most teachers are guided, if not directed, by a set of state, provincial, district, or school standards that set the expectations for student learning at a given grade level. Additionally, we have assessment data on what our students know and can do at a given point in time. It is our job as teachers to align this information with classroom instruction and assessment. Unfortunately, not all standards are clear and specific enough to be useful for daily classroom instruction. In planning a curriculum, we want to articulate goals and expectations that are specific, measurable, and appropriate to the grade level of the students (Conzemius & O'Neill, 2006). It is much easier to align instruction and assessment when we know exactly what we're striving for.

Unit Planning for a Balanced Writing Program

Of all the types of planning that teachers do, Kenneth Moore (2009) suggests that unit planning may very well be the most important. Effective unit planning enables teachers to present related content and skills in a seamless and sequential fashion over an extended period of time. It provides an opportunity for teachers to determine what standards or objectives will be taught and then organize and present instruction in a way that meets the needs of the students in their classes.

Traditionally, unit planning was subject-specific, based on a broad topic or concept related to that content area. Recent years, however, have seen the rise of the cross-curricular, integrated unit. Although there is merit to integrating various content areas' standards under the umbrella of a common theme (Ronis, 2008), writing frequently gets shortchanged. All too often, writing becomes simply a tool for learning rather than a learning goal in itself. If we want our students to become better writers, we must build units of study

FIGURE 2.1. A Sample Year's Genre-Based Writing Curriculum

Month	Lesson Focus
September	Personal narrative (and launching the writing workshop)
October	Research report (often integrated with a content area study)
November	Procedural writing
December	Free-choice writing workshop
January	Persuasive writing
February	Descriptive writing
March	Poetry
April	Free-choice writing workshop and/or test writing
May	Fictional narrative
June	Multigenre project[a]

[a]As described in *The Write Genre: Classroom Activities and Mini-Lessons That Promote Writing With Clarity, Style and Flashes of Brilliance*, by L.J. Rog & P. Kropp, 2004, Markham, ON, Canada: Pembroke.

around learning to write as well as writing to learn. Units of study in writing may focus on various themes or aspects of the writer's craft or the writing process, but I prefer to organize the year's writing units around key genres and text forms (Rog & Kropp, 2004). A genre-based unit generally requires about four to six weeks, so a year's curriculum might look something like the schedule presented in Figure 2.1.

The Six Traits of Effective Writing

One of the most widely used resources for planning and implementing a balanced writing program comes from the six-traits model, developed by teachers and researchers from Northwest Regional Educational Laboratory (NWREL). Based on Paul Diederich's (1974) research on criteria for good writing, the traits have been identified as follows:

- Ideas
- Organization
- Voice
- Word choice
- Sentence fluency
- Conventions

Although *six traits* has become a commonly used generic term, NWREL introduced the copyrighted term *6+1 Traits* in 2002 to include the trait of presentation, or the appearance of the text on the page.

The six traits have always been part of good writing. The work of NWREL serves to define the traits in a balanced framework that is accessible and useful for teachers and students. All too often, we have allowed writing instruction to be dominated by conventions, agonizing over misspellings and marking every missing punctuation mark. The six-traits framework reminds us that conventions are only one slice of the pie in good writing—an important slice, to be sure, but no more tasty than the ideas, structure, voice, words, and fluency of the piece.

Over 25 years ago, when the NWREL team began developing this framework, they determined that the best way to make the traits useful for teachers and students was

Six Traits of Effective Writing

- **Ideas and content** looks at focus and development of topics and details. Any idea can be turned into a piece of writing. Effective writing demands rich detail and strong elaboration.

- **Organization** refers to the logical flow and order of details. Good organization hooks the reader with an engaging lead and wraps up the piece with a satisfying conclusion. Teaching the structures of different genres and text forms will help students learn to organize their work in ways that are appropriate to the topic and purpose for writing.

- **Voice** involves a combination of style, tone, mood, purpose, and connection to the audience. Effective writing speaks to a reader and creates an emotional connection between the reader and the text. Often, voice is the product of all the other traits: the details and how they are organized, the choice of words, and the flow of the sentences.

- **Word choice** is about the language a writer uses to craft ideas, convey a message, or paint pictures in a reader's mind. This trait encourages writers to experiment with interesting word combinations and figures of speech.

- **Sentence fluency** refers to the rhythm and cadence of the language. The only trait to focus on the way writing sounds rather than what it means, sentence fluency is best achieved by varying the lengths, types, and structures of sentences. It's also about putting words together in ways that sound good to the ear.

- **Conventions** are the mechanics of writing: spelling, punctuation, capitalization, and grammar. Australian children's book author Mem Fox describes conventions as the "good table manners of written language" (as cited in Culham, 2003, p. 214); they exist as a courtesy to help readers negotiate the print.

to describe how each of the traits looked at various degrees of proficiency. Hence, the first six-traits rubrics were developed initially as assessment tools for helping teachers appraise the strengths of a piece of writing and determine where it might be taken next. Since that time, an entire model of instruction has sprung up around the six traits. This framework provides us with a common language for teaching, conferring, and evaluating; facilitates instruction at the point of need; and serves as a constant reminder to balance the writing program.

The Four Basic Steps for Using the Six-Traits Framework
1. Choose the genre or text form that will be the focus of the unit.
2. Determine a set of learning objectives for the unit around each of the six traits.
3. Plan a sequence of lessons to address each of the learning objectives.
4. Create an assessment plan and construct a rubric that is aligned with your learning goals.

Planning a Genre Unit Using the Six-Traits Framework

The six-traits model is not a program. There are many different ways for teachers to use its components to meet the needs of their students and their program. Some teachers plan units around each of the traits individually. I prefer to integrate all of the traits into each genre-based unit. I find the six-traits framework to be a powerful organizer for balancing instruction and ensuring that I am addressing all aspects of writing. In fact, every minilesson in this book is linked to one or more of the traits. Planning a genre unit using the six-traits framework involves four basic steps:

1. *Choose the genre or text form that will be the focus of the unit.* Often, grade groups of teachers choose to plan collaboratively, creating a year's writing curriculum of common units that may be connected to topics of study in content areas or special events in the school, such as Earth Day or an oratory contest. Most state, provincial, and district jurisdictions mandate the study of certain text forms at each grade level. Once we've selected the genre for the unit, it's often helpful to build a framework that links the genre to each of the traits. Table 2.1 lists a set of questions to answer as we create a framework for the text form.

2. *Determine a set of learning objectives for the unit around each of the six traits.* Learning goals are the foundation for both instruction and assessment. The "Goldilocks principle" is the challenge here: not too many and not too few, but "just right." Organizing the learning objectives around the six traits helps balance instruction and address all of the elements of good writing. My rule of thumb is two or three objectives per trait; otherwise, the unit becomes unwieldy and doesn't allow the students enough time to master the objectives. The trait of conventions is somewhat distinct from the others in that the objectives are less likely to be genre-based and more likely to arise

TABLE 2.1. Sample Questions for Creating a Six-Traits Framework for a Genre Unit

Trait	Characteristics of the Text Form
Ideas	• How does the writer find topics for this writing? • What kind of details and elaboration will be used?
Organization	• How are the details organized? • Are there any unique text structures or formats?
Voice	• What is the purpose for writing? • Is there a specific tone or mood? • Are there special techniques for creating that mood?
Word choice	• What kinds of words does the writer use? • Are there literary techniques that are appropriate to this theme?
Sentence fluency	• What types of sentences does the writer use? • Are there special ways to convey the rhythm and sound of the writing?
Conventions	• Are there any conventions unique to this form? • Based on district standards and student assessments, what conventions are appropriate for this unit?

out of the needs of the students. As you construct the unit around the traits, be sure to consult your state, provincial, or district curriculum for mandated objectives and align them with your own classroom assessments of your students.

3. *Plan a sequence of lessons to address each of the learning objectives.* It's not necessary to reinvent the wheel in order to create lesson plans. There are 40 of them in this book alone, not to mention in many other print and Internet resources. For instance, ReadWriteThink.org is an excellent source for lesson ideas. Most teachers already have a repertoire of terrific teaching tools up their sleeves but are always looking to adapt ideas from other sources to meet the unique needs of their students and their circumstances. The key is to focus on what students are learning as writers rather than a clever activity or cutesy assignment. Look for lessons that meet specific learning goals. As you plan your lessons, consider the best order of presentation. Do some lessons serve as prerequisites for others? Is there a step-by-step component that should be considered? For example, in Chapters 5 and 6, I have carefully laid out a sequence of minilessons that build on one another to go from planning to drafting to revising a piece of informational and persuasive writing.

Be sure to build in some flexibility in timing to allow for the "teachable moment." And, of course, be prepared for repeating lessons to achieve a particular objective; our students don't always get it the first time around! Fortunately, the structure of the writing workshop lends itself to empowering each student to work at his or her own level, but consideration should always be given to accommodating individual differences.

4. ***Create an assessment plan and construct a rubric that is aligned with your learning goals.*** How will you know whether students have achieved the learning goals? Will you define degrees of mastery? Will you evaluate drafts and guided writing tasks as well as published work? Is there a process as well as a product component in the evaluation?

When I evaluate students' progress to determine a report card grade, I will look at my anecdotal notes and their writing logs to review their use of writing time. I examine drafts and published writing for evidence of the strategies the students have been taught, such as revision for vivid verbs or adding showing statements to telling statements. I sometimes give them a writing "test," such as a piece of writing to revise for writer's craft or to plan a "stars and wishes" peer conference (see Chapter 4). Usually, I create a rubric to help me assign scores to different levels of proficiency.

The rubric is the best tool we have for assessing various aspects of writing. There are plenty of rubrics—six-traits and otherwise—available online and in print resources, but these are rarely aligned with the specific objectives and instruction in our classrooms. The bottom line is that rubrics are most effective for both teaching and assessing when they are constructed to match the learning objectives. Even when teachers choose (as I do) to construct the rubric collaboratively with the students, it's good to have a plan in mind. We should never expect our students to undertake anything we haven't tried ourselves.

There are several decisions to make in developing a rubric: How many levels will there be? Will grades (or a range of grades) be attached to each level for the purpose of evaluation? In addition to meeting the product goals of the unit, what about the process goals? Many teachers use an ongoing yearly rubric to assess aspects of student growth in process. Of course, it must be noted that we should not assess anything that has not been explicitly taught in the unit.

A Few Thoughts on Rubrics

Rubrics are wonderful tools for assessment and instruction in many different areas where proficiency is difficult to quantify. Nowhere is this more evident than in writing. A rubric is a particular type of rating scale that describes one or more criteria at different degrees of quality. Rubrics not only help us evaluate writing, but they also help us see (and guide students in) what must be done next to improve a piece of writing.

In his 1988 analysis of the research on writing assessment, Richard Stiggins noted that teachers spent at least 20% of their professional time in assessment-related activities, but in most cases, neither the students nor the teachers themselves could articulate the specific criteria by which the writing was evaluated! Because the evaluation of writing can be so subjective, many teachers resort to focusing on surface features that are either "right" or "wrong." It's much easier (and perhaps safer) to note spelling errors and missing punctuation than it is to grade idea development or voice. In fact, Brian Huot (1990) found that the two criteria most closely associated with high scores in writing were the length of the paper and a lack of spelling errors. Furthermore, individual bias can impact the grade that a piece of writing receives. It's hard to avoid being influenced by a touching topic, a special turn of phrase, or even the quality of the handwriting. Huot has gone so far as to suggest that writing scores may actually tell us more about the scorer than the writing!

Rating scales were first introduced by Diederich (1974) to help teachers evaluate writing more accurately and impartially. He found that providing teachers with rating scales not only resulted in more consistent and reliable scores but was also a much quicker grading method. Whereas it previously took teachers an average of eight minutes to score each paper, when using rating scales, it took them less than two minutes per paper.

If a rubric is to be useful, it must be aligned with our specific learning objectives. Websites like RubiStar (rubistar.4teachers.org) are tools for helping teachers build their own rubrics. Ideally, we can work collaboratively with students to construct rubrics in language they understand. Constructing or sharing the rubrics with students builds independence and self-evaluation. When they understand the criteria for quality writing, it helps both their initial drafts and subsequent revisions (Hillocks, 1986). When students understand what is expected of them, they are better able to determine the extent to which their own writing meets those expectations and make changes to improve it.

I often play "the scoring game" with intermediate students, in which we collaboratively assess anonymous pieces of writing and score them. Often, students will then be given the opportunity to revise those pieces of writing to try to raise the scores. It's amazing how much easier it is to revise someone

Guidelines for Developing Rubrics

1. *Determine how many levels your rubric will contain.* Rubrics commonly have four to six levels, although they can have as few as three or many more.

2. *Select the criteria you want to assess.* Criteria on the rubric should be aligned with the learning objectives in the unit.

3. *Determine what level is the "standard."* In my opinion, there is no need for more than one degree of inadequacy, although others have made strong arguments in favor of showing students how close they are to achieving the standard.

4. *Create a description of each of the criteria at each level.* An excellent rubric is descriptive enough to clearly distinguish each level from the next without leaving gaps between the levels. Try to use specific and descriptive language. General terms like *more* or *stronger* and subjective terms such as *creative* or *effective* may not be clear to either the evaluator or the one being evaluated. However, beware of limiting yourself by being too specific, such as "three details…." Are three mundane details superior to two excellent ones? Also, try to avoid combining two or more criteria into one description, as this creates a challenge when a writer has achieved one criterion but not the other.

5. *Decide how the rubric will be used for grading.* Are all of the criteria weighted equally? Will you assign a score or a range of scores to each level? How will the rubric align with report card grades?

else's writing! When students have an opportunity to work in collaborative groups to assess pieces of writing, they are more likely to internalize the knowledge and apply it to their own writing. When they are invited to work with others to revise a piece of writing by an anonymous writer, they are able to experiment with writing in a low-stakes, nonthreatening environment. They learn how to choose words that make writing more powerful, how to add detail to enhance a theme, and how to prune unnecessary information, building skills that we hope will transfer to their own compositions.

A Sample Unit Plan

Figure 2.2 provides a sample narrative unit plan, developed by teachers of grades 3–5 at an elementary school in western New York, who dedicated one of their summer professional development days to collaborative planning in writing. We worked together, using the process just described, to articulate learning objectives, plan lessons, and construct a rubric for the unit. For some of the teachers, starting with learning objectives rather than lesson activities represented a shift in thinking. Others observed that it was a challenge to go "deep" rather than "wide," in other words, to limit the number of learning goals in order to allow for mastery. For example, we decided to dedicate several days to the trifold planner (see Chapter 3), requiring students to complete three planners before turning any into a draft. The teachers agreed that the collaborative professional experience was both educational and time-saving in the long run.

Because the school district requires that all students have a piece of narrative writing in their portfolios by mid-October, the teachers chose to construct a six-week unit of study on narrative writing. Figure 2.2 includes their selected learning objectives, lesson sequence, and assessment rubric. In developing the rubric, we decided to describe levels 5, 3, and 1, with the understanding that writing that surpassed one level but did not quite attain the next could be assigned 2 or 4. (This also satisfies the universal teacher penchant for the plus or minus.) We also felt that it was important to use language that students could understand, so the rubric could be used for self- and peer assessment, as well as teacher conferences and evaluation.

If assessment is to be truly integrated with instruction, it must be continual and ongoing—a starting point rather than an endpoint in the instructional process. Continual monitoring of student learning means that the lines between assessment and instruction fade to a perpetual cycle of assessing student progress toward educational goals and adapting instruction to help foster that progress.

FIGURE 2.2. Sample Unit of Study on Narrative Writing

Objectives for Personal Narrative Writing

Trait	Framework	Learning Goal: Students will be able to…
Ideas	• The topic is from the writer's personal experience.	• Choose topics from their own experiences. • Include interesting details that stick to the topic and tell the complete story. • Elaborate on key details.
Organization	• The text flows chronologically, in the order that the events happened.	• Organize details with a beginning, middle, and ending.
Voice	• First person is used. • The text tells a story.	• Maintain a consistent first-person voice. • Use snippets of dialogue.
Word choice	• There is descriptive vocabulary, such as vivid verbs.	• Energize their writing with vivid verbs.
Sentence fluency	• There is a combination of long and short sentences with varied sentence types.	• Incorporate at least one question and one exclamation into the text. • Use simple and compound sentences correctly.
Conventions	• These are determined by assessment.	• Spell high-frequency words correctly and complex words with logical invented spelling. • Capitalize and punctuate sentences correctly.

Lesson Sequence

Week	Lessons
1	• What is a personal narrative? (read a mentor text) • Finding topics (writing ideas bingo) • The Trifold Planner (beginning, middle, and end; complete three)[a]
2	• Modeling and practicing trifold planners continued • Turning a plan into a draft (complete two drafts) • Using the first person • Putting ideas in sentences • Listing Versus Layering[b]
3	• Vivid Verbs (revise drafts)[c] • Dabble in Dialogue[b] • Dialogue 2 (quotation marks) • Star and wish peer conferences[b]
4	• Self-editing • Polish and publish

[a]See Chapter 3. [b]See Chapter 4. [c]See Chapter 7.

(continued)

FIGURE 2.2. Sample Unit of Study on Narrative Writing (*continued*)

Assessment Rubric

Trait	5	4	3	2	1
Ideas	This writing stays on topic and is full of interesting details and elaboration.		This writing stays on topic and has lots of interesting details.		This writing seems to wander a bit and is missing important details.
Organization	This writing has a beginning that grabs the reader's attention, an interesting middle, and an ending that wraps the piece up neatly.		This writing has an interesting beginning, middle, and end. The details flow in an order that makes sense.		This writing is hard to follow. Some of the details seem to be out of place.
Voice	I can hear this writer's voice tell the story.		This writing sounds friendly but pretty much all the same.		This sounds like robot writing, a bit choppy and flat.
Word choice	This writing is full of wow words, especially vivid verbs.		There are some wow words in this piece, including a few vivid verbs.		The words in this piece are pretty ordinary.
Sentence fluency	A variety of long and short sentences, including questions and exclamations, make this writing sound rhythmical to read.		This writing contains lots of simple and compound sentences and at least one question and exclamation.		What sentences?
Conventions	All of the words (except maybe a few difficult ones) are spelled correctly. Sentences have capitals and ending punctuation.		Most of the ordinary words (except maybe a few difficult ones) are spelled correctly. Most sentences have correct capitals and ending punctuation.		There are so many mistakes in spelling and sentences that it's hard to read this piece of writing.

CHAPTER 3

The Power of Prewriting

My house is pretty spotless when I'm writing: no crumbs in the knife drawer, carpets vacuumed, baseboards dusted. So, what does that tell you about me? That I'm a neat freak? I love to clean for relaxation? No, it probably means that I've hit writer's block. For me, drafting is the hardest part of the writing process. No matter how excited I am about a topic, no matter how ready I am to convey my ideas, it is always a struggle to get those first words down on paper. That's why I can always find lots of ways to avoid writing. I certainly can't sit down to draft if there are crumbs in the cutlery drawer or dust bunnies under the beds! However, I have found a prescription for the pain of getting started: a good prewriting plan.

Many intermediate-grade students have the same problem. Even when they have a topic in mind, they just can't get started. Often, they just need some planning tools to put in their writing toolboxes. The Carnegie Corporation of New York's meta-analysis of research on writing found that teaching prewriting strategies is one of the most valuable aspects of writing instruction (Graham & Perin, 2007). This report indicates that engaging students in activities for generating and organizing details before writing improves the overall quality of the writing.

A good prewriting plan always makes drafting easier and revising more manageable. When the draft has been planned ahead of time, it is usually more clear and coherent, because the writer can work on crafting ideas rather than creating them. Best of all, prewriting usually prevents that most deadly of all revision activities: ripping it up and starting over. Prewriting plans are not carved in stone; they are simply tools for generating and organizing ideas. Writers frequently change their minds as they write, eliminating some details, adding and changing others. That's why some writers say that "prewriting" is a misnomer; they return to their plans over and over during all stages of the writing process, often revising and adjusting the plans as they go.

When I teach a new prewriting strategy, I have the students practice at least two or three plans before turning any of them into drafts. I want the students to try out the strategy enough to be able to use it independently— and, in my experience, one shot is never enough. When I'm confident that the majority of my students have mastered a particular prewriting strategy to my satisfaction, I'll offer some instruction on converting the plan to a first draft. I'm often surprised at how many intermediate students don't know how to draft. Instead, they often turn the writing into little more than a regurgitation of the words in the planner. As you model, don't hesitate to let students see you changing, deleting, and inserting details, that is, *revising as you write*. A prewriting plan is just a map; it doesn't prevent you from taking a side road now and then to explore new sights. You'll return to the highway eventually, but you may have made discoveries along the way that could change your life—or at least your piece of writing.

The seven minilessons in this chapter are intended to provide tools to fill our students' prewriting toolboxes (see Table 3.1 for an overview of the minilessons in this chapter). Each minilesson offers a twist on a traditional strategy: research-based but tweaked to best meet the needs of students in intermediate grades. From choosing topics to generating and organizing details, each minilesson offers a tool or technique for helping students get over those initial hurdles of the writing process.

"I don't know what to write about" may very well be the most common chorus in writing classrooms. On occasion, teachers will have a purpose for providing a prompt or specific assignment for writing, but if we always provide topics for writing, our students will never learn to write for themselves. Research and good practice have shown that when students choose their own topics, their writing shows greater quantity *and* quality (Graves, 1994). In fact,

TABLE 3.1. The Power of Prewriting Minilessons at a Glance

Minilesson	Page	Trait(s) Addressed	Lesson Focus
Love It or Loathe It	33	Ideas	Using likes and dislikes as topics for writing
Get in the Loop!	35	Ideas	Freewriting to generate ideas and build fluency
TAP Into Writing	38	Ideas, voice	Considering topic, audience, and purpose before writing
Storm and Sort	41	Ideas, organization	Brainstorming and categorizing ideas before writing
Tell It Twice	43	Ideas, organization	Pretelling to generate and organize ideas before writing
The Trifold Planner	45	Ideas, organization	Organizing writing by beginning, middle, and end, with appropriate details
Mind Mapping	49	Ideas, organization	Creating a visual to organize writing

Graves goes so far as to say that if students have trouble thinking of ideas to write about, they're not writing enough! The more opportunities writers have, the easier it will be for them to think of ideas. My husband, Paul Kropp, is the author of over 50 novels for teens and preteens, as well as books for parents and teachers, but he says he won't live long enough to write all the ideas in his head! People who write a lot learn to see writing topics everywhere they look.

That said, we sometimes need to provide a framework for young writers to use for topic generating. It's always a good idea to "keep a topic in your pocket," in this case, the front pocket of the writing folder. There are many ways to create topic lists. In our book *The Write Genre: Classroom Activities and Mini-Lessons That Promote Writing With Clarity, Style and Flashes of Brilliance* (Rog & Kropp, 2004), we offer a "bingo card" of sentence stems that can be turned into topics for writing. Another easy approach is a list of "fantastic fives," such as

- Five people, dead or alive, whom I would like to meet
- Five of the most important inventions of all time
- Five of the most interesting or unusual animals, birds, or fish
- Five things my school should change
- Five of the best things about being a kid
- Five interesting places I have visited or would like to visit

One of my favorite topic-generating activities may be found in **Love It or Loathe It**. This is simply a T-chart on which students list their favorite and not-so-favorite things and use them as springboards for a wide range of writing pieces. This is a good minilesson to use early in the year as an introduction to writing workshop. Each day, students choose one of their topics for a short writing piece. By the end of the week, I have a collection of first-draft writing pieces that I can use to assess what my students know and can do in writing, and to plan future instruction.

Get in the Loop! is a minilesson that uses freewriting to help students generate ideas, build fluency, and find topics that may be developed into writing pieces. Freewriting (Elbow, 1973), or quickwriting (Jacobs, 1986; Rief, 2003), is a technique that involves writing nonstop for a period of time, putting on paper whatever words come to mind. Writers choose (or are given) a topic and write for a fixed time period of several minutes without stopping to reflect, craft, change words, or fix spelling. Freewriting has three basic features:

1. Concentrate on content.
2. Don't worry about form.
3. Write without stopping.

Freewriting builds fluency by freeing up writers from worries about conventions, craft, and even coherence, and helps them "stimulate their thinking so that they can find words" (Rief, 2003, p. 8). Linda Rief quotes Joel, an eighth grader, as saying, "'Quickwrites help me write down some things I didn't remember I knew'" (p. 8). Once those initial words are in front of a writer in black (or blue or whatever) and white, the rest often comes much easier. Frequently, the seeds of ideas for further writing can be found in a freewrite. At other times, the freewrite simply opens the floodgate of more ideas.

Looping is a variation of freewriting in which writers loop from one freewrite to another, using a word, phrase, or idea from one freewrite as the stimulus for the next (Cowan & Cowan, 1980). Not only does this activity help students come up with ideas for writing, but also it is a good writing warm-up for many writers who struggle to get those initial words on paper. Elbow (1973) maintains that daily freewrites are the best way to build writing proficiency. One might say that a freewrite a day can keep writer's block away.

TAP Into Writing invites writers to consider not just what the writing will be about but also who will read it and why. The acronym *TAP* stands for topic, audience, and purpose. TAP is adapted from the RAFTS strategy (role, audience, format, topic, and strong verb) developed by Carol Santa (1988) and her colleagues as both a prompt-generating tool and an approach to refining a writing topic. Who is our reader and how do we want him or her to respond to the writing? Do we want to congratulate or criticize, amuse or tug at the heartstrings, inform or entertain? The decision about audience and purpose will affect the details we include, the words we choose, and the tone we use in the writing. When writers turn on the TAP, their writer's voice is more likely to pour out.

Once writers have selected a topic for writing, they need to produce and organize the details that will be included. Brainstorming is a time-honored technique for idea generating and is well supported by research in effective teaching (Marzano, Norford, Paynter, Pickering, & Gaddy, 2001). The rules for brainstorming are standard, whether the setting is an intermediate classroom or a corporate boardroom: Come up with as many ideas as possible without judgment or revision, with out-of-the-box thinking and piggybacking on previous ideas encouraged.

Although brainstorming can be an excellent means of generating ideas on a topic, it sometimes leads to disorganized, stream-of-consciousness writing. The minilesson **Storm and Sort** requires writers to list as well as organize ideas by encouraging students to sort their details, combine those that fit together, and consider the order in which they should appear, not to mention taking a critical "re-view" of the details to eliminate those that will simply not fit into the organized whole. The use of different-colored highlighters adds a visual and kinesthetic component to the process. In my companion book, *Marvelous Minilessons for Teaching Beginning Writing, K–3* (Rog, 2007), I suggest that primary writers should brainstorm each detail on a separate slip of paper and then physically manipulate the slips to sort the details. If your students have not had a lot of experience with brainstorming, you may want to start with this process.

As James Britton once said famously, "Talk is the sea upon which all else floats" (as cited in Allen, 2009, p. 41). All too often in intermediate grades, we limit talk instead of encouraging it. Yet, writing should be nested in talk (Writing Study Group of the NCTE Executive Committee, 2004). We talk to one another during peer conferences, teacher conferences, and minilessons. "As they grow, writers still need opportunities to talk about what they are writing about, to rehearse the language of their upcoming texts and run ideas by trusted colleagues before taking the risk of committing words to paper" (Writing Study Group, 2004, para. 41).

Talking before writing helps writers clarify their thinking, organize their ideas, and consider how best to convey their message. Talking about one's writing invites others to ask questions and offer suggestions, and allows the writer to revise before the composing process even begins. The minilesson **Tell It Twice** affords intermediate students a unique opportunity to pretell what they are going to write, not once but twice, with different partners. By the time the writers have voiced their ideas, they have the details more complete in their minds and can dedicate more mental energy to putting the ideas on paper. Pretelling is often combined with other prewriting techniques; students may generate a written plan first, then tell someone else about it before starting to draft. Either way, articulating ideas before writing can make drafting easier and revision less painful.

Graphic organizers have been recognized as a powerful prewriting tool for generating, organizing, culling, and categorizing ideas for writing (Gallick-Jackson, 1997). Graphic organizers are visual or pictorial tools for arranging ideas in a particular order or showing relationships among bits of information. They help writers create a big picture into which they can file new details and information. Graphic organizers assimilate new information with existing knowledge, creating a mental filing cabinet that enables writers to sort, sift, and share information. There are many different organizers for prewriting, and it's a good idea to provide students with a range of options from which to choose. One of the most versatile graphic organizers is **The Trifold Planner.** This three-part foldable teaches students to organize both the big ideas and the supporting details before writing. Writers start by summarizing the beginning, middle, and end, then they add details to each section. This planner also includes a section for planning opening and closing statements for the writing piece. Although the trifold is a linear type of planner, it can be used for organizing any form of writing into three parts.

Mind Mapping introduces another form of graphic organizer, in which writers combine pictures and text in planning a piece of writing. The mind map was first introduced to the business world in the mid-1990s as a brain-based technique for fostering creativity and enhancing memory (Buzan, 1993). Its use has become widespread in educational circles for generating, organizing, and recalling ideas in the language arts as well as other school subjects. A traditional mind map looks like ideas radiating from a central topic, and each of those subordinating ideas supports a starburst of supporting details. Ideas are represented in visual form, as pictures, symbols, icons, or other graphics, supported by labels and minimal text. Howard Gardner's (2004) classic research on multiple intelligences reminds us to honor the diversity of learning strengths and styles in our classrooms. The mind map is a great tool for visual learners.

Helping our students stock their writing toolboxes with a repertoire of prewriting tools is an important step in the writing process. A strong plan makes drafting easier and reduces the need for revision. It does not limit creativity or oblige the writer to stick to a prescription; it simply enables him or her to begin with the end in mind, not only shaping the piece more effectively but also enabling the writer to devote more energy to the crafting of the piece. Good writing starts with a good plan. Different writers and different writing tasks require different types of plans. This chapter offers a collection of minilessons for helping student writers stock their prewriting toolboxes.

Love It or Loathe It

Here's a great way to get started with writing in that first week of school! Students need to learn that the best writing comes from topics they care about. What's better than something we absolutely love or absolutely loathe?

Learning Goal: Students will be able to generate writing topics that they have strong feelings about.

Trait: Ideas

Introduction: Tell students that the best writing comes from topics that a writer feels strongly about. In this lesson, they will have an opportunity to generate a list of things they absolutely love and things they absolutely can't stand. It may be necessary to define the word *loathe* for the students, but it could be a great addition to their vocabulary! Later, they can tuck this list into the "Ideas" pocket of their writing folders to be available as topics for writing. The "loves" and "loathes" can lead to equally strong feelings and strong writing.

Instruction: Model, model, model! Even something as simple as a two-column chart should be demonstrated before students are expected to tackle it on their own. Make a T-chart by folding a piece of paper in half. Label one half "Love It" and the other half "Loathe It." In each column, generate a list of objects, food, places, activities, habits, hobbies, and beliefs that you adore or abhor. (My only rule is no people's names in the "Loathe It" column.) As you write, talk through your thinking for the students. My modeling appears in Figure 3.1.

FIGURE 3.1. Sample Love It or Loathe It Lists

LOVE IT!

- cinnamon buns
- Italy
- bike riding
- singing
- blue sky
- my babies

LOATHE IT!

- olives
- Daylight Savings time
- traffic
- cell phones in public places
- littering

Guided Practice: Guide students in creating their own T-charts and encourage them to list four or five items in each column. After writing, have them share their lists with a partner. Invite students to add more ideas to their charts after the partner talk.

After students have had an opportunity to make and share their lists, revisit your own lists and do another think-aloud. Talk about how you might turn these topics into writing pieces.

I could write a comparison of jazz and rap music and tell why I prefer one over the other. I could write a travelogue or personal narrative about my trip to Italy. I could even write a research report on Italy or maybe how to make Italian ice cream, which is called gelato. I could write an explanation of daylight saving time and why it doesn't work for me. Any of these items on either list could be my writing topic!

In my think-aloud, I try to model a range of topics and genres and let students know how a broad topic like "ice cream" can turn into a specific topic like "how gelato is made." Have students return to their writing partners and talk about ways that they could turn some of the items on their lists into topics for writing.

Independent Application: Have students choose one of the ideas from their Love It or Loathe It lists and use it as a topic for writing.

Get in the Loop!

Freewriting (also known as quickwriting) is a strategy that writers use to warm up, build fluency, and generate ideas. Writers simply write nonstop for a certain time frame, without worrying about spelling, conventions, sentence structure, or even clarity and craft. When writers "loop," they choose a "nugget"—a word, phrase, or idea from the original freewrite—and use it as the starting point for another freewrite.

Learning Goal: Students will engage in the freewriting and looping strategy and use it as a starting point for further written exploration.

Trait: Ideas

Introduction: Introduce the idea of a warm-up. Students who play sports or music may know about the concept of doing some sort of exercise to get your mind (and body) ready for an activity. Tell students that they will be doing a writing warm-up in this lesson that will help them get their minds and writing fingers ready for writing. They will be "getting in the loop" with professional writers by learning a fun technique called freewriting.

Boys and girls, I think today you will learn the easiest writing strategy you have ever tried! It's called freewriting, and it's just that—free! You don't have to worry about sentences or spelling or capitalization or even making sense. The only rule in freewriting is you can't <u>not</u> write! You just write and write and write until you're told to stop. Sometimes you'll write sentences, sometimes you'll just write random words, and sometimes you might even write "I don't know what to write" until something else comes to your mind. Lots of professional writers use this technique to help them warm up or bust that writer's block that we've talked about. The amazing thing is that out of all this mess, most writers can find a sparkling idea, a nugget of gold, buried deep in the mess of words that can loop to another piece of writing.

Instruction and Guided Practice: Provide students with the four basic rules for freewriting:

1. You can't *not* write. You have to keep writing something, anything, until the time is up.

2. You must write in a forward motion only. You can't erase, cross out, change, revise, or even go back and reread.

3. You don't have to stick to the same topic. Piggyback on other ideas. Make connections. Change your mind.

NOTES

Date

_____

_____

Observations

_____

_____

_____

_____

_____

_____

_____

_____

_____

_____

Notes for Future Instruction

_____

_____

_____

_____

_____

_____

_____

_____

_____

_____

4. If you want to use a period, do it. If you don't want to, don't. Spell words as well as you can, as long as *you* can read them later. Write long sentences or short sentences, with punctuation or without. The main point here is getting free-flowing words and ideas down on paper.

Show the students the example in Figure 3.2 or create one of your own. (You may even want to save a couple of your students' samples to show future classes—with the writers' permission, of course.) Point out that there are some complete sentences and some sentence fragments. Sometimes I just used a word or group of words—one idea just led to another.

Provide a topic or have students choose their own. The sample Love It or Loathe It T-chart (see page 33) is a good source of topics. Sometimes a famous quote like "The love of money is the root of all evil" or "Practice makes perfect" can be an inspiration. Even just copying the quote can get the writing going.

Set the timer for a specified period of time. I find that three minutes works for starting out with intermediate students; monitor your own students to judge their stamina. When the timer buzzes, they must stop writing. I find that having students count the words they've written is often an incentive to write more the next time. You might want to give a 20-second warning to allow students to complete a word or thought.

FIGURE 3.2. Freewriting Example

Ice cream. Love it. Not every kind of ice cream, mostly soft ice cream. Vanilla. Kind of boring, isn't it? Some people say vanilla is dull, like white bread. There's also gelato. Now that's a treat. Mmmm. A delicious cross between sorbet and ice cream. Creamy like ice cream but tart flavors like sorbet. I like limone (lemon) or frutta di bosco (fruit of the woods). Stracciatore has streaks of chocolate. I'm getting hungry. When is lunch? I think I'd like—

Next comes the looping part. Students must reread what they've written and highlight at least one word, phrase, or idea that they think might be a nugget for future writing. They now use that nugget as the starting point for another freewrite. This time, add another 30 seconds to the time limit to extend their writing stamina.

You might want to extend to a third loop, even if it's on a subsequent day. The freewrite may turn out to be the stimulus for a new piece of process writing. Consider offering a follow-up demonstration, using bits and pieces of your freewrite in a more connected and coherent piece of writing.

Independent Application: Have students turn and talk about how and when they might use freewriting in their own writing process. Encourage them to take a timer and allow themselves a timed freewrite and loop for an independent writing warm-up or to bust that writer's block.

Date

Observations

Notes for Future Instruction

TAP Into Writing

Choosing a topic is the first step in planning a piece of writing. When writers consider their reader and purpose for writing as well as the topic, the writing tends to be more focused, energetic, and interesting. This lesson uses the acronym *TAP* for topic, audience, and purpose.

Learning Goal: Students will be able to identify the topic, audience, and purpose for a piece before writing.

Traits: Ideas, voice

Introduction: Remind students that they already have a number of ways to generate topics for writing, but there's more to getting ready for writing than just thinking about a topic. Tell students that they will learn about focusing their topics by considering the reader and the purpose for writing.

Think about the way you talk to your friends on the playground. Maybe you call them by nicknames and even insult them in a joking way. You wouldn't talk to your teacher or principal in the same way. You would probably call them "Mr." or "Ms." and use a more respectful tone. Has your mother ever said to you, "Don't use that tone of voice with me!"? Well, just in the same way that you use different tones of voice for talking to different people, you use different tones of voice in writing for different readers. If we don't think about our voices when "talking" to a reader in our writing, then it sometimes sounds a bit like reading the dictionary! In this lesson, you're going to practice thinking ahead about your topic, your reader, and your reason for writing. We call that TAP: topic, audience, and purpose.

Instruction: Display the statements in Figure 3.3. Have students turn and talk to a partner about who the audience for each one might be. If you

---

FIGURE 3.3. TAP Audience Examples

- Thanks a lot for the joke book you sent me for my birthday. It's hilarious! Every year, you always manage to figure out exactly what I like. Love you lots!
- I am writing to request a copy of the free magazine you advertised on your website. It looks like something I will need for a school report. Please send it to the address below.
- It's my birthday party! Please come Tuesday at 4:00! Bring your swim suit.
- Once upon a time, there were three bears: a mommy bear, a daddy bear, and a baby bear, just like you!

TAP = topic, audience, and purpose.

think your students might have trouble with this task, provide them with the following choices: little kid, a museum website, Grandma, a friend. Ask the students how they can distinguish different audiences (readers) and purposes for a piece of writing.

Remind students of the acronym *TAP*. They can TAP into writing by planning the topic (what the writing is about), the audience (who the reader will be), and the purpose (the reason for writing).

Although you don't always know who is going to read your writing, thinking about who might read it or whom you would like to read it helps you decide what details to include and what tone of writer's voice you will use. Sometimes writing is addressed to a specific reader, like your grandmother, the principal, a friend, or a magazine. We sometimes refer to our reader as the "audience." Other times, a reader might be more general, such as a small child, another student, a business, or an adult. Thinking ahead about the purpose of the writing also helps you focus your writing— and even helps you decide what text form the writing will take. The purpose is why you are writing. What do you want your reader to take away from this writing? Do you want them to be entertained, informed, invited, or thanked?

Together, build an anchor chart with a list of purposes for writing, such as the one in Figure 3.4.

Guided Practice: Provide students with the TAP Prompts reproducible at the end of this minilesson; note that all of the prompts on one chart will have the same topic, but the audiences and purposes will vary. Divide the students into four groups so that each will respond to a different prompt. Afterward, have students share their writing with a small group to hear how the voice and tone vary according to the audience and purpose.

Independent Application: Tell students that they should think about the topic, audience, and purpose for every piece of writing they do. Follow up as you confer with students in independent writing.

FIGURE 3.4. Sample Anchor Chart of Purposes for Writing			
amuse	describe	inspire	tell a story
announce	encourage	invite	tell how to
ask, inquire	entertain	persuade	thank
complain	explain	recount an event	
compliment	give an opinion	relay news	
criticize	inform, teach	suggest	

TAP Prompts

	Topic	Audience	Purpose
1		People on a diet	Bragging about resisting temptation—or admitting that they didn't
2	Description of a piece of chocolate cake	Young children	Lecturing on why it's bad for you
3		Diners in a restaurant	Persuading them to order it for dessert
4		Friends having dinner	Complaining about how bad it tasted

Storm and Sort

Brainstorming is a time-honored technique for generating ideas for writing. However, although brainstorming may help a writer develop a lot of details, it doesn't do much to help the writer organize them. As a result, writing that goes directly from brainstorming to drafting often appears to be a mishmash of ideas that don't always flow smoothly for the reader. I like to add another step between brainstorming and drafting: sorting the brainstormed details. In this lesson, students use different-colored highlighters to sort brainstormed details into groups.

Learning Goal: Students will be able to brainstorm and organize details on a topic before writing.

Traits: Ideas, organization

Introduction: Remind students about the practice and purpose of brainstorming as a prewriting tool for helping them generate possible details on a topic. By the intermediate grades, most students will have had experience with brainstorming. They may generate more details than they choose to use in the writing piece and will often spontaneously elaborate on some details when they begin to draft; both are good practices for writers to learn and should be modeled in minilessons. In this lesson, students will learn about planning a piece of writing by generating as many details on a topic as possible and then organizing those details before starting to draft.

Instruction: Choose a topic, then model and think aloud your brainstorming of possible details. You may want to use the list of ideas for a town fair in Figure 3.5 as the basis for your think-aloud.

I've brainstormed a bunch of things I do and see and eat at the fair. Now that I have lots of details, I have to think about how I might organize them. I could number them in the order that I would do them when I go to the fair, but that often comes out as a "breakfast to bed" kind of list. I think I'll put these details together in groups that belong together. For example, I'm going to highlight all the details that have to do with food in yellow. Then I know that when I draft my piece, I will be able to put all these details together in a paragraph.

Model highlighting the food details. Invite the students to work with you to sort and highlight the remaining details with other colors. Logical groupings might be "rides" and "exhibits." Have students turn and talk to a partner about where details like the fireworks or carnival games might fit.

FIGURE 3.5. Brainstormed Ideas for a Town Fair

- Cotton candy
- More fried food on fair day than all the rest of the year put together!
- Strange fried foods, like chocolate bars, Oreo cookies, and turkey eggs, along with our usual French fries, onion rings, and corn dogs
- Favorite rides that spin but aren't too high
- Tilt-a-whirl, merry-go-round, and scrambler
- Exhibits of strange products that chop food, clean eyeglasses, or make hamburger patties
- Prize-winning pies, crafts, and preserves
- Rides first, then food
- Ice cream on a stick rolled in peanuts
- Beautiful baby contest (every baby wins a prize)
- Fashion show
- Double Ferris wheel and roller coasters
- Corn on the cob dipped in a big vat of butter
- Big prizes on display but only little plastic things awarded
- Gathering at the midway for fireworks at the end of the night

Guided Practice: Have students collaboratively brainstorm a dozen or so details on the topic of "why fourth [or fifth or sixth] grade is the best." Then, they can work in pairs to sort the details into groups.

Independent Application: Have students choose a topic (the Love It or Loathe It T-chart on page 33 is a good source). Storm and sort at least 10 details about the topic. The students can put this sorted list into the "Topics" pocket of their writing folders to use for a future writing piece.

Tell It Twice

Most student writers need to talk during writing and before publication, conferring with their teacher and peers. Talk is also important before writing. The pretelling strategy involves sorting, sifting, and organizing details orally before putting pen to paper. This lesson invites students to pretell their story, plan, or details to a partner, then regroup and tell their ideas again to a different partner. This exercise gives young writers the opportunity to consolidate their thinking, leaving more energy to devote to putting the words on paper.

Learning Goal: Students will be able to use pretelling to plan a piece of writing.

Traits: Ideas, organization

Introduction: Open with a discussion of why writers prewrite. Tell students that in this lesson, they will be practicing one of the easiest kinds of prewriting: pretelling. In other words, they will be telling someone else what they're going to write about before they put the words on paper.

Instruction and Guided Practice: Remind the students about the importance of talk in the writing workshop.

Talking is an important part of writing workshop. You talk to other people while you're writing, and you have writing conferences before you publish. You might try out your ideas on someone else and get questions or advice from them about how to make your writing more interesting and clear to a reader. In this lesson, you're going to practice talking to someone before you even draft your writing, as a way to collect and sort and organize your ideas as well as get your thinking clear in your own mind.

Have students select a topic from one of their topic lists. Make sure each student has a partner. For this exercise, each partner has a time limit (usually about three minutes, but I monitor the conversations and adjust accordingly) to tell the partner about his or her topic and invite some questions or feedback from the other partner.

Give the students a few minutes to think about their ideas and make some notes, if they choose. After the first telling, students will work with new partners to tell the same story again. In most cases, writers solidify their choice of details, the organization, and even the words they use during the second telling, which makes it easier to write the piece later.

Date

Observations

Notes for Future Instruction

Date

Observations

Notes for Future Instruction

This strategy may be combined with any other written prewriting strategy. Students can write their plan before the first telling to formulate their thoughts. After the first telling, the students have an opportunity to return to their writing tables, reflect on their telling and their partners' observations, and make any necessary adjustments to their written plans before repeating the telling process with another partner.

Partner Sticks

In order to group students randomly, I use craft sticks that have a different color or sticker at the bottom of each, with two of each color or sticker. Each student draws a partner stick from the cup, checks the bottom of the stick, and is partnered with whoever draws the matching color or sticker. In this way, students must work with a variety of different people, and no one is left out.

Independent Application: Invite students to reflect on the "tell it twice" strategy and consider how pretelling might be useful for them in their writing. Tell students that they may use this strategy for a new writing piece.

The Trifold Planner

This organizer is not as exotic as the name might imply. A trifold is a piece of paper folded into three equal parts. We hope that our intermediate students have already had plenty of practice organizing their writing into beginning, middle, and ending sections. This organizer's strength is the support it gives the writer in planning key details for each section. It helps writers ensure that all the key information is in place and unnecessary details are omitted. This tool lends itself neatly to narrative writing (personal or fictional) and is also adaptable to informational writing. More sophisticated writers will also use the trifold to plan their openings and closings on horizontal folds at the tops and bottoms of the pages.

Learning Goal: Students will be able to plan the beginning, middle, and end of their writing as well as generate key details for each section.

Traits: Ideas, organization

Introduction: Review what students know about stories having a beginning, middle, and end. Tell students that they will learn a simple organizer for planning the beginning, middle, and end of a piece of writing, using a trifold (a fancy word for a paper folded in three). This organizer is best introduced during the reading block as a tool for retelling a story. Start by summarizing the beginning, middle, and end of the story, then insert the appropriate details in each section. It makes a very effective graphic organizer for retelling.

Instruction: Use a piece of chart paper folded into three columns, or a suitable alternative for enlarged text (see the reproducible at the end of this minilesson). Demonstrate for students how to fold a paper in thirds, then how to use the trifold planner to prewrite the beginning, middle, and end of a personal narrative story. As an alternative to folding, use the graphic organizer on page 48. Figure 3.6 is a sample of a completed planner.

In the first column, write a sentence that summarizes the beginning of your story. Then, do the same with the middle and end of your plan in the second and third columns. Talk about your plans as you are composing them in the planner.

After talking about the "big picture," discuss which key details you will put in each column. Jot these down, along with any interesting or special words or phrases you might include in your writing. Writing out these details in complete sentences now is optional.

Date

Observations

Notes for Future Instruction

NOTES

Date

_____

Observations

_____
_____
_____
_____
_____
_____
_____
_____

Notes for Future Instruction

_____
_____
_____
_____
_____
_____
_____
_____
_____
_____
_____
_____
_____

FIGURE 3.6. Sample Trifold Planner

Julie and I snuck out of the house and down to the slough.	We poled the raft out to the middle of the slough, but the raft sank.	We sat in the tree house all afternoon waiting for our jeans to dry.
• We were 10 years old and not allowed to go rafting on the slough. • We had to get past my aunt's watchful eye. • The slough was a dirty old pond where cows drink.	• The raft was an old, waterlogged door, and the pole was a broom handle. • We stepped gingerly onto the raft. • As we poled to the middle, the raft sank farther into the water. • The freezing water came up to our ankles then our knees. • By the time we got to the middle of the slough, the raft was almost touching the bottom, and we were in water to the middle of our thighs.	• Our jeans were soaking wet to midthigh. • We couldn't go into the house this way. • We took off our jeans and hung them in the tree house. • We sat in the tree house, shivering in our skivvies all afternoon. • It was a cold fall day, the temperature not much above freezing.

This planner takes some time to master, but the effort is worthwhile as it is a versatile prewriting tool. I teach the students to summarize the beginning, middle, and end before adding the supporting details. I sometimes require a minimum number of details, such as two for the beginning, four for the middle, and two for the end. As with any new strategy, I have the students complete at least two or three planners before turning any into a draft, so they master the use of this tool before refocusing the writing. At that point, I find I have to demonstrate how to turn a plan into a draft, showing students how we flesh out details as we transform them into connected text. Only when students are capable of completing the beginning, middle, and end portions of the planner do I introduce a top and bottom fold for planning an introduction and conclusion.

Guided Practice: Walk students step by step through the process of folding the paper and completing the planner:

1. *Choose a topic. (If students do not have a "topic in their pocket," so to speak, one that works well is "how I got this scar.")*

2. *Use the trifold planner to write one sentence each for the beginning, the middle, and the end of your story.*

3. *Turn and talk to a partner about your beginning, middle, and end. Have your partner ask you questions about each part. This will help you plan the details you need in each section.*

4. *Add at least three details to each section.*

Independent Application: Students should complete at least two or three planners on different topics. Ultimately, they will choose one of the planners to transform into a draft.

Extension: When students have mastered this planner, introduce adding a one-inch horizontal fold to the top and bottom of the page. These will be used to plan the opening and closing of the piece.

Date

Observations

Notes for Future Instruction

Trifold Planner

Mind Mapping

Mind mapping is another type of graphic organizer that uses visuals to represent relations among ideas. This prewriting tool combines words with pictures, symbols, icons, and other visuals to represent ideas and details for writing. It enables writers to fuse pictures and words to generate, organize, sort, and prioritize information in preparation for writing. This minilesson uses a radial style mind map, which is best for descriptive writing. It is easy to adapt the format of the mind map to chronological, compare/contrast, cause/effect, procedure, or other text structures.

Learning Goal: Students will be able to create a visual mind map as a planner for writing.

Traits: Ideas, organization

Introduction: Review previous work on prewriting strategies and graphic organizers. Tell students that in this lesson they will be learning about another type of planner called a mind map (see Figure 3.7). Show the students a sample of a traditional road map and talk about the connections between it and a prewriting mind map.

FIGURE 3.7. Sample Mind Map on Snails

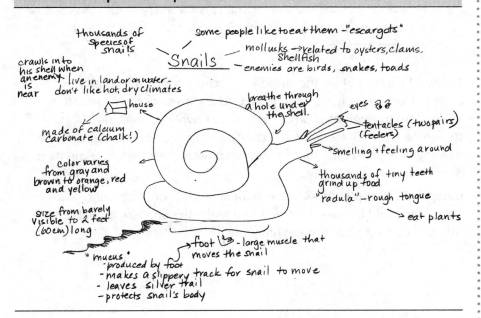

Boys and girls, you have done a lot of work with graphic organizers for writing and for other subjects. Today, you're going to learn about another kind of organizer called a mind map. Think about what we use maps for. They help us visualize where one place is in relation to another place. They give us a big picture of an area or region. They tell us where one space ends and another begins. Perhaps most important, they guide us in getting from one place to another. A mind map does the same things for a writer. It helps us visualize the pieces of the writing and guides us as we work through the writing. Just like a road map is a combination of words and symbols, our prewriting mind maps will combine pictures and print.

Instruction: Model as you explain the rules for this type of mind map:

1. Start with a blank piece of paper.

2. In the center of the page, draw a picture or symbol to represent the main idea, theme, or topic of the writing. Label it with a working title.

3. Around the outside of the central picture, draw additional labeled sketches of ideas that might be included with this topic. Join them to the main idea with lines.

4. Feel free to extend lines outward as you think of supporting details related to the main idea.

5. Include as many ideas as you want. You can always sort and sift them later.

6. Use numbers or arrows to put the ideas in the order that you might want to use them in your draft.

7. Remember that this is a tool for writing, not a pretty picture. The visuals are just sketches to help you remember ideas; they don't need a lot of elaboration and detail.

Guided Practice: Have the students choose a topic from their Love It or Loathe It lists or assign a topic related to a current content area study. Walk them through the completion of a prewriting mind map step by step. After they have completed their mind maps, use the "tell it twice" strategy to explain their mind maps to someone else before using them to draft a piece of writing.

Independent Application: Have students reflect on their mind maps and how they could be useful for drafting. Make this strategy available to students as they plan future writing pieces.

CHAPTER 4

Elaboration: Adding Details to Details

Ludwig van Beethoven started with four famous notes (*DA-DA-DA-daaa*) to compose the *Fifth Symphony*. Leonardo da Vinci elaborated on a series of pencil sketches to create the *Mona Lisa*. The arts are full of examples of how elaboration can turn a basic idea into a masterpiece, and writing is no exception.

In describing her inspiration for the book *Girl With a Pearl Earring*, Tracy Chevalier (n.d.) states on her website,

> I was lying in bed one morning, worrying about what I was going to write next. A poster of the Vermeer painting Girl With a Pearl Earring hung in my bedroom…. I lay there idly contemplating the girl's face, and thought suddenly, "I wonder what Vermeer did to her to make her look like that. Now there's a story worth writing." Within three days I had the whole story worked out. (para. 1)

That's the power of elaboration: taking a basic idea and extending, expanding, enriching, embellishing, or refining it.

Too often, our intermediate students produce narratives that are little more than "breakfast to bed" stories—lists of chronological details without development, all receiving the same amount of attention and importance. Good writing is so much more, and that *more* is often elaboration. Elaboration clarifies and expands, sending a message to the reader about which ideas are most important and interesting. Elaboration can let a writer slow down the reading to build suspense, or take the reader galloping on a whirlwind of exciting emotions and events.

Elaboration is all about the development of ideas. It means adding subordinate information, illustration, or examples that clarify or expand key ideas, in other words, adding details to details. Elaboration may be as simple as inserting an adjective to modify a noun or as intricate as telling a story to illustrate a point.

Educational research tells us that there is a correlation between the quantity and quality of elaboration and the overall effectiveness of a piece of writing (Hendrickson, 1980). However, simply adding more words to a piece of writing doesn't necessarily make it better. Students need to learn not only what elaboration is but also when to use it. Not all details merit elaboration; writers elaborate on only the most important or interesting ideas. Stephen Benton and Paul Blohm (1988) identified layers of elaboration as the top-level (main) ideas that form the premise of the text; the mid-level ideas that further explain, define, or describe a top-level idea; and the base-level ideas that provide specific examples or supporting details.

In his classic study on criteria for writing, Diederich (1974) finds that the most powerful indicator of effective writing is the quality of the ideas: "their richness, soundness, clarity, development, and relevance to the topic and the writer's purpose" (p. 6). As teachers, we often advise students to "tell me more," "add more details," or even "elaborate on that" without giving them the tools in their writing toolboxes to enable them to choose which details to elaborate on or how to develop those details most effectively. The seven minilessons in this chapter are intended to do just that (see Table 4.1 for an overview of the minilessons in this chapter).

The first step in using elaboration effectively is deciding which details to elaborate on. While some students write laundry lists of details without developing any of them, other students clutter their writing with multiple modifiers or bog it down with minutiae of every detail, regardless of how

TABLE 4.1. Elaboration: Adding Details to Details Minilessons at a Glance

Minilesson	Page	Trait(s) Addressed	Lesson Focus
Listing Versus Layering	55	Ideas, voice, word choice	Elaborating on selected details
Tell Me More: Powerful Peer Conferences	59	Ideas	Conferring to guide elaboration
Don't Tell Me, Show Me!	62	Ideas, word choice, conventions	The "show, don't tell" strategy
Make a Splash With the Senses	65	Ideas, word choice	Adding multisensory details
Add an Anecdote	68	Ideas, organization, voice	Expanding on an idea by telling a story
Tell It in Slow-Mo	71	Ideas, voice, word choice	Slowing down the most exciting part
Dabble in Dialogue	94	Ideas, voice, conventions	Inserting dialogue for interest and voice

insignificant. As Barry Lane (1993) asks, "How do we teach students to discriminate between the purposeful and the extraneous? How do we teach them that details are not wallpaper but walls?" (p. 22).

The first minilesson, **Listing Versus Layering**, illustrates the difference between writing that lists and writing that layers. When we layer in writing, we choose key details to develop and describe. This lesson is intended to help young writers decide which ideas are important enough to elaborate on and guide writers in adding layers of supporting details.

Many students have trouble seeing their writing from someone else's point of view. They know what they intend to say but don't realize that the reader doesn't have access to what's going on in the writer's head. That's why student writing may have gaps in information or missing details. Teaching students to confer with peers in a meaningful way helps the writer see his or her writing from the point of view of a reader—and helps the reader engage more critically with the writing. **Tell Me More: Powerful Peer Conferences** teaches students to conduct "star and wish" student-to-student conferences. Based on the TAG conference described in Chapter 1, this minilesson teaches peer readers to help each other identify strengths of their writing (stars) as well as details that merit more expansion or explanation from a reader's point of view (wishes).

When students can identify which details in their writing merit elaboration, they need some tools for adding description and expansion. **Don't Tell Me, Show Me!** focuses on the "golden rule" of writing: Telling statements simply pass along a piece of information, whereas showing statements draw the reader into the text, inviting him or her to participate in constructing meaning from the text. Showing can add voice, tone, and style to an otherwise bland detail. "My mom was really mad" does not evoke the same image as the following example:

> At the sight of the mess all over the kitchen, Mom's nostrils flared, and her face slowly turned red. She took a deep breath. And in that calm and very quiet voice that always forecast trouble, she said the words we were dreading to hear, "You boys are toast."

By showing us what Mom looked like, did, and said, I have tried to paint a mind picture that conveys much more than just telling the reader that Mom was *really* angry. Don't Tell Me, Show Me! is not just about details but also about word choice and grammatical construction. Telling statements generally use the verb "to be" (*is, are, was, were, am*), whereas showing statements often (though not always) use more vivid verbs.

When we think about showing instead of telling, we think of using our eyes instead of our ears. But what about our other senses? Tastes, smells, and textures can also create images in the reader's mind. In **Make a Splash With the Senses**, students will practice using sensory details as an elaboration technique. This minilesson approaches the creation of sensory images by inviting students to elaborate on sights, sounds, smells, tastes, and textures evoked by ordinary concepts such as colors.

Another way to elaborate on an idea in writing is to tell a short story or give an example to illustrate a point. **Add an Anecdote** teaches students to relate a brief account of an experience or an example to give the reader more detail. Anecdotes can add voice and personality to a piece of writing, because they often elicit an emotional response from the reader. This minilesson also teaches students to back up a general statement with specific examples.

It may be hard to believe, but slowing down the most interesting part of a narrative can actually make it more exciting. **Tell It in Slow-Mo** uses the technique of describing the minutiae of an event, as if it were occurring in slow motion. Slow-motion writing lets the reader in on all the details of a critical event: actions, the setting, and even feelings. By slowing the action down, the writer sends the reader the message that this event is worthy of his or her time and attention.

Another way to elaborate on a key idea is to include short snippets of conversation, as in **Dabble in Dialogue**. Dialogue can support elaboration and idea development in a variety of ways, from defining characters to building background information. Dialogue rarely moves the plot forward, but should add voice and interest to the writing and be used judiciously and purposefully. Otherwise, it starts to sound like a *Seinfeld* script—talk about nothing! This minilesson teaches students to convert ordinary conversation into book language as well as to add tag lines and punctuation.

These seven minilessons offer just a few of many techniques that writers use for elaborating, embellishing, clarifying, and developing important ideas in their writing. In Chapter 6, we look at additional techniques for supporting ideas in persuasive writing. Once students know how to develop ideas, they can focus on crafting those ideas in more artful ways.

Listing Versus Layering

Some student writing consists of a virtual laundry list of ideas or events, each receiving the same amount of attention and space in the text. This lesson teaches students to distinguish between listing and layering, and to be able to choose which details merit more elaboration.

Learning Goal: Students will be able to distinguish between listing and layering, and identify the details that require elaboration.

Traits: Ideas, voice, word choice

Introduction: Read and display the two fourth-grade writing samples in Figure 4.1. You may want to have the students discuss what makes the second piece of writing more interesting to read, or directly explain to the students that the second piece of writing is more interesting because the writer has given us details about the details.

FIGURE 4.1. Fourth-Grade Student Samples of List Writing Versus Layered Writing

List Writing

My Trip to Disneyland

I went to Disneyland with my brother, grandparents and cousins. We checked into our hotel and the next day we went on all the rides. They had a light parade, we watched it at night. My favorite ride was Star Tours. We also went on the Pirates of the Caribbean and Haunted Mansion. I liked Splash Mountain too. The next morning we went to Notsberry Farm. We went swimming in a large pool. We went home the very next day.

Layered Writing

My Memory

I have a lot of memories but my favorite memory was my trip to Disney World. My whole family had a blast. The rides, the shows and meeting all the characters was so fun. I liked Star Tours. You sit down and buckle your seat belt and watch a movie screen while the room spins. But my favorite ride was Splash Mountain. First I would wait in line full of excitement. Then I would get in a log with butterflies in my stomach and then ride through the story. Soon I would go up the hill and all of a sudden I went whooshing down with the water splashing in my face and frogs jumping in my stomach. It was so much fun and that's probably why I went on it five times! I loved that trip and it's a memory I'll never forget.

Date

_____

Observations

_____
_____
_____
_____
_____
_____
_____
_____
_____
_____
_____

Notes for Future Instruction

_____
_____
_____
_____
_____
_____
_____
_____
_____
_____
_____
_____
_____

These pieces of writing are both about similar topics, but the writing styles are quite different. The first piece is just a list of all the things the writer did at Disneyland, but it doesn't really tell us much about any of those things; in fact, we don't know why Star Tours was the writer's favorite or even what Star Tours is! The second piece of writing is more interesting to read, because the writer elaborated on some of the rides. Elaborating means telling more; when we elaborate, we add details to details to make our writing more interesting and easy to understand. In today's lesson, you are going to learn about elaboration in writing.

Instruction: Revisit the two sample texts to discuss what techniques the writer has used to elaborate on his or her ideas, such as the following:

- Focused on only a few attractions rather than listing all of them
- Described how the rides worked
- Included feelings and emotions
- Showed instead of told
- Used vivid verbs such as "whooshing"
- Used figurative language such as "frogs jumping in my stomach"

Remind the students that effective writing comes in layers rather than lists. Layered writing focuses on only a few key ideas and gives *layers* of details. Some of the ways that writers elaborate on details is by providing descriptive details, describing feelings, and using powerful words.

The reproducible at the end of this minilesson provides an example of list writing. Invite students to participate in composing a sentence or two of elaboration on one of the details, or think aloud as you model an example yourself. It's easy to demonstrate revision on a word processor. With handwritten text, you might have to "stretch the paper" by cutting and pasting in additional paper or using "spider legs" to point to another spot on the page where additional information might be added. An example of this is shown in Figure 4.2.

Guided Practice: Provide students with a copy of the "Fun Foods at the Fair" text from the reproducible at the end of this minilesson. Have them work in pairs to use spider legs to add elaboration to at least one more detail in the passage.

Independent Application: Ask students to revisit one of their existing drafts to revise by inserting one or more elaborative details to an existing idea.

FIGURE 4.2. List Writing Sample, Edited

Fun Foods at the Fair

One of my favorite things to do at the summer fair is eat! I could eat all day, starting with minidonuts in the morning, followed by a mid-morning snack of candied apple or maybe a chocolate covered banana. For lunch I like to eat a big slice of pizza and ice cream on a stick. By afternoon, I'm ready for a corn dog and I always leave room for fudge. I usually have fish and chips for dinner, but I can never go home without a final feast on a sugary funnel cake.

→ My mouth starts to water at the mere thought of those creamy and crunchy taste sensations of vanilla ice cream dipped in chocolate and rolled in peanuts. It's a little taste of heaven in the middle of the fair grounds.

Fun Foods at the Fair

One of my favorite things to do at the summer fair is eat! I could eat all day, starting with minidonuts in the morning, followed by a midmorning snack like a candied apple or a chocolate-covered banana. For lunch, I like to eat a big slice of pizza and ice cream on a stick. By afternoon, I'm ready for a corn dog, and I always leave room for fudge. I usually have fish and chips for dinner, but I can never go home without a final feast on a sugary funnel cake.

Tell Me More: Powerful Peer Conferences

Peer conferences (see Chapter 1 for a detailed description) can be powerful learning experiences for both the writer and the reader. The writer learns to see his or her writing from a reader's point of view, and the reader learns to read more critically and thoroughly. This lesson focuses on teaching students to engage in "stars and wishes" peer conferences. The stars are compliments about the piece of writing, and the wishes are suggestions for "tell me more." The challenge for students is to develop the language to speak empathetically and effectively about another student's writing. This lesson provides instruction and practice in successful peer conferences.

Learning Goal: Students will be able to identify strengths (stars) and areas that require more elaboration (wishes) in a peer's writing.

Trait: Ideas

Introduction: Talk to the students about how hard it can be to see your own writing from the point of view of a reader.

When I'm writing something, I know in my head all of the background information I need to understand the words on the page. But, sometimes I forget that my reader doesn't have the same background knowledge that I do, so he or she might not understand everything in my writing. By asking questions of a writer, I can let him or her know what parts I, as a reader, might not understand or need more clarification on. In this lesson, you're going to learn how to have those conversations with a writer. We call them "peer conferences." A peer is someone who is at the same level you are—not an expert or a teacher, but a reader just like you.

Instruction: An effective conference has two parts: a compliment and a question or suggestion. That's why these conferences are called "stars and wishes." We always start with something positive: an interesting detail, a clever turn of phrase, or a powerful lead. It's important that this comment is specific, focused, and particular to the *writing* (as opposed to the *writer*). Comments like "This is good" or "You know lots about the topic" don't really help the writer with his or her writing. Instead, we say, "Your introduction really grabbed my attention," or "Your writing is full of rich details that stick right to the topic."

The "wish" is a question, point of confusion, or desire for elaboration. In these conferences, we are going to use the stems "I wish you would

NOTES

Date

_____

Observations

_____
_____
_____
_____
_____
_____
_____
_____
_____

Notes for Future Instruction

_____
_____
_____
_____
_____
_____
_____
_____
_____
_____
_____
_____

tell more about..." and "I wish you would explain...." Notice that the wish is not judgmental. Students have to learn that this is not a criticism of the piece, and they need to be careful about the writer's feelings. The wishes do not evaluate the quality of the writing but simply ask for clarification or elaboration. This is not the time to talk about punctuation or spelling; the focus is on the idea development of the piece. Of course, as students develop the language to discuss other elements of writer's craft, such as word choice or voice, these can be included in the peer conferences, but this lesson focuses exclusively on "tell me more."

Demonstrate a peer conference for the students or invite them to share their stars and wishes. Figure 4.3 is a piece of fourth-grade writing called "People and Paper Clips Don't Mix" to use as a model.

If I were having a "tell me more" conference with this writer, I'd start by saying some great things about this piece of writing. Her opening grabbed my attention. I like the way she inserted a question near the end. She used some good descriptions like "huge fingers" and "puny little mouth." She put the details in an order that makes sense.

Now, I need to figure out what I want to know more about. I don't need to know more about every detail, like what the room was like or what the cousin's name was. I am wondering, Can you tell me more about why two little kids were playing when everyone was asleep? Can you tell me more about how your uncle knew that you were in trouble? Two questions are probably enough for this piece of writing. Now it's time for the writer to decide what information she needs to add to the piece in order to make it more clear to a reader.

Guided Practice: Display a sample piece of writing such as Figure 4.4, "The Magic Crystal Ball," and have students turn and talk with a partner about their stars and wishes. Have students share their ideas to ensure that the comments are appropriate and productive.

Independent Application: Have students select a piece of their own writing for a peer conference. Put students in pairs to confer with one another. Require that they make at least one revision to their own writing following the peer conferences.

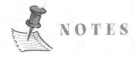

FIGURE 4.3. Sample Fourth-Grade Writing for Tell Me More

<u>People and Paper Clips Don't Mix</u>

Once I did something that I'll never do again. My cousin and I were playing in my brother's room. Mostly everybody was asleep. We were just toddlers at the time. I found a paper clip and I put it in my mouth. I swallowed it and it got stuck in my throat. I started to choke out blood. My uncle was up though and heard me. My mom and aunt and my big brother woke up. Then my uncle came to the room and put his huge fingers into my puny little mouth. He felt it, got a grip on it and pulled it out. Then we all went to the hospital to see if there were any more paper clips in my mouth. But there weren't any more. My uncle actually saved my life. And do you know what? My dad slept through the whole thing!

FIGURE 4.4. Sample Student Writing for Peer Conference ("Stars and Wishes")

<u>The Magic Crystal Ball</u>

Long, long ago in a faraway land, there lived a king, a queen, a princess, and a prince. The princess had a magic crystal ball. One day, an evil archduke captured the princess and stole the crystal ball. The next day, Prince Brody came to the rescue. On the way, he had to fight a fire-breathing dragon. When Prince Brody struck the dragon, it disappeared. Prince Brody then entered the castle. He sneaked past the evil archduke. He got the key and entered the chamber where the princess was. Prince Brody and the princess went looking for the magic crystal ball and the magic knife. They found the ball and the knife and returned to the castle. Then, the princess lived happily ever after.

NOTES

Date

Observations

Notes for Future Instruction

Don't Tell Me, Show Me!

"Show, don't tell" has been called the golden rule of writing, and it's certainly one most fiction writers live by. This lesson uses the book *The Dirty Cowboy* by Amy Timberlake (2003) as a model of showing rather than telling, and invites students to replace or elaborate on telling statements with more descriptive showing details.

Learning Goal: Students will be able to create interesting showing details to supplement or replace telling statements in their writing.

Traits: Ideas, word choice, conventions

Introduction: Here's an opportunity to bring out your inner drama queen (or king). Surprise the students by storming into the classroom with an angry expression on your face, flailing your hands or making fists, and making a few statements like, "I can't believe it! This is ridiculous!" in a furious voice. Then, stop and step back into your normal persona.

How did I feel just then? How did you know? I didn't need to tell you that I was really angry, because I showed you with the expression on my face, my gestures, the words I said, and how I said them. Just like the scene I acted out for you, one thing we know about good writing is that it's more effective when it shows us rather than tells us. Today you're going to have a chance to practice showing rather than telling in your writing.

Instruction: Read the first four pages of *The Dirty Cowboy* (and display them on a document projector, if possible), inviting students to listen for details that *show* that the cowboy is dirty.

Here's an example from a book we've read before, <u>The Dirty Cowboy</u> by Amy Timberlake. In this book, the author shows us how incredibly filthy the dirty cowboy is without ever using the word <u>dirty</u>!

Create a "five-finger" planner (trace or photocopy a hand shape) on a piece of chart paper, the overhead projector, or other writing surface that is visible to all of the students. On the "palm" of the hand shape, write the telling statement, "The cowboy was dirty." Have students contribute showing details from the text.

Talk about the kinds of details (for example, comparisons) and words, such as alliteration and vivid verbs, that the writer used in her showing statements, as in Figure 4.5. Depending on the sophistication of your students, you may want to point out that telling statements always use

FIGURE 4.5. Sample "Five-Finger" Planner

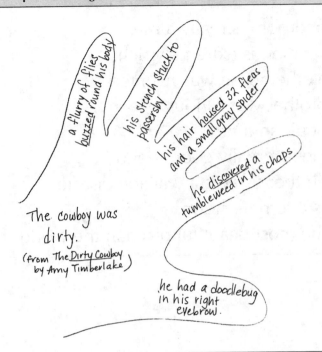

a flurry of flies buzzed 'round his body!

his stench stuck to passersby

his hair housed 32 fleas and a small gray spider

he discovered a tumbleweed in his chaps

The cowboy was dirty.
(from The Dirty Cowboy by Amy Timberlake)

,he had a doodlebug in his right eyebrow.

the verb *to be*, whereas showing statements tend to have more vivid verbs. Highlight the verbs in Timberlake's showing details.

With the students, choose one of the telling statements from the list in Figure 4.6 and have them turn and talk to a partner, creating some possible showing statements. Display a five-finger planner and write the telling statement on the palm of the hand. Invite students to share some showing details that support the telling statement and record them on the planner.

Guided Practice: Have students work in pairs or small groups to create their own "show, don't tell" planner. They can select one of the telling statements in Figure 4.6 and complete a five-finger planner with showing statements. (More sophisticated writers may be required to include a vivid verb in each detail.)

Independent Application: Instruct students to go back into a piece of their writing and highlight a telling statement. Have them revise by replacing or adding to the telling statement with two or more showing statements.

Date

_____
_____

Observations

_____
_____
_____
_____
_____
_____
_____
_____
_____
_____
_____

Notes for Future Instruction

_____
_____
_____
_____
_____
_____
_____
_____
_____
_____
_____
_____
_____

FIGURE 4.6. Samples of Telling Statements

- My bedroom is really a mess.
- That person is extremely rich.
- I think the house was haunted.
- My brother was furious.
- My pet is so funny.
- He/she is a really good friend.
- My brother/sister is a walking disaster.
- It was a terrible storm.
- It is the most beautiful place in the world.

Make a Splash With the Senses

Descriptions of smells, tastes, sounds, and textures can be unique and effective ways to elaborate on an idea in writing. It's easy to use tastes to describe feasts or sounds to describe trains, but this minilesson uses the poetry book *Hailstones and Halibut Bones* by Mary O'Neill (1961/2009) to inspire students to create sensory images for everyday concepts such as colors.

Learning Goal: Students will be able to elaborate on a key idea or detail with sensory images.

Traits: Ideas, word choice

Introduction: Tell students that showing rather than telling isn't just about visual images. Some very effective elaboration can come from using the other senses as well.

When we think of creating images, we usually think of visual images, pictures in our mind, but we can also create images of smells, tastes, sounds, and textures. It's fairly easy to write about smells and tastes when we describe a Thanksgiving dinner, or of how the cold water feels when we dive into the lake on a sunny summer morning. In this lesson, we're going to think about associating smells, sounds, tastes, and textures with ordinary things like colors.

Instruction: If possible, as you read the book *Hailstones and Halibut Bones* (O'Neill, 1961/2009), display the text that conveys smells, sounds, tastes, and textures as related to colors. Pause frequently to talk about unusual images that the writer has used, such as, "White is the beautiful / Broken lace / Of snowflakes falling / On your face" (p. 29).

As a shared writing exercise, choose a color and invite the students to brainstorm as many sensory images as they can. You can start with a basic color such as purple or choose a more exotic paint chip color. The senses chart in Figure 4.7 was a collaborative effort of a fifth-grade class based on a paint chip color called Caribbean coral.

Guided Practice: Suggest that students work in pairs on this task. Gather a collection of paint chips from your local paint store and put them in a gift bag. Have each pair draw a chip from the bag as their color for creating a senses chart. (You can use the reproducible at the end of this minilesson.)

Date

Observations

Notes for Future Instruction

Date

_____

Observations

_____
_____
_____
_____
_____
_____
_____
_____
_____

Notes for Future Instruction

_____
_____
_____
_____
_____
_____
_____
_____
_____

FIGURE 4.7. Sample Fifth Graders' Senses Chart

Color	Looks Like	Sounds Like	Smells Like	Tastes Like	Feels Like
Caribbean coral	• Weathered brick on an old house • Mixing pink and orange	A trumpet with a mute (wa-wah)	• Wet, sandy beaches • Smoldering embers as a fire is dying down	Cantaloupe juice dripping down your chin	• Rough stone with bumpy, pointy parts like coral • Warmer than pink but cooler than red

Look at the color and its name. Think about the images it conveys. Write the color name in the first column.

Work with your partner to fill in the senses chart in the handout, brainstorming two or three sensory images for each sense. Remember, with brainstorming, we write down all ideas, not just the best ones. After you're done, you'll have a chance to choose the most creative or interesting images.

Independent Application: Have students choose a piece of writing from their writing folders and revise it by inserting at least one appropriate sensory image.

Extension: Have students turn their senses charts into free-verse poems about a color. Think aloud as you choose, adapt, and manipulate images from the class chart (such as the one in Figure 4.7) into a poem. Then, have students use their charts to create poems of their own.

Senses Chart

Color	Looks Like	Sounds Like	Smells Like	Tastes Like	Feels Like

Date

_____

Observations

_____
_____
_____
_____
_____
_____
_____
_____
_____
_____

Notes for Future Instruction

_____
_____
_____
_____
_____
_____
_____
_____
_____
_____

Add an Anecdote

An anecdote, or brief story, is one of the most engaging tools that writers can use to support an idea or make a point. Telling a story adds voice, passion, and personal involvement to a piece of writing. This minilesson uses a piece of student writing and an excerpt from a novel as models of using examples or anecdotes to elaborate on key ideas, and reinforces the skill of telling a story briefly and effectively.

Learning Goal: Students will be able to write anecdotes that effectively support statements and ideas in their writing.

Traits: Ideas, organization, voice

Introduction: With the students, talk about why elaboration is important in writing. You may want to review techniques they have already learned for elaboration. In this lesson, they will be learning about adding an anecdote to elaborate on an idea. An anecdote could be funny, as in a joke, or quite poignant. Writers add anecdotes to prove a point, support an idea, or add voice and interest to a piece of writing. The following is an example from *Ghost House* by Paul Kropp (2003):

> We were together in preschool, friends in grade two and best buddies since grade six.... If there is a problem, then all of us have to fix it. Like the time Hammy's line drive smashed Mrs. Headly's window. We all chipped in on that one. After all, it was my baseball, A.J.'s bat and Zach's pitch that got the ball going. We are that tight. (pp. 6–7)

Instruction: Distribute the example of student writing called "My Friends" in the reproducible at the end of this lesson. Compare this piece with the excerpt from *Ghost House*. In the *Ghost House* piece, the author makes a statement ("If there is a problem, then all of us have to fix it."), then follows with a short example—an anecdote. In the "My Friends" piece in the handout, the writer makes lots of statements but never gives us examples or stories to elaborate on them.

Let's look at this sixth-grade piece called "My Friends." According to this writer, what do we know about friends? I'm wondering what the writer means by "they're there when I need them" and "doing stuff I might regret later in life"? One of the problems with this piece of writing is that the writer gives us lots of general statements, but she's missing specific examples. One way she could make her writing better is by telling what she means when she says her friends were "there when I need them" or telling about a time her friends stopped her from "doing stuff I might regret later in life." Today you are going to work on elaborating in writing by adding an anecdote, or a quick story. An anecdote can make a point, add personality, or simply support an idea in the story.

Ask the students to locate general statements in the student sample in the "My Friends" handout. One example is "they're there when I need them." Invite students to turn and talk to a partner about possible examples and anecdotes to elaborate on this statement. Demonstrate for the students how you might stretch the paper (cut the page apart and tape in an extra paper) to insert an anecdote for elaboration, as in Figure 4.8.

Guided Practice: Provide students with a copy of the piece "My Friends." Have them work in pairs to insert a possible anecdote to one of the other general statements.

Independent Application: Have students use a piece of writing in their writing folders to revise by adding an anecdote.

FIGURE 4.8. Anecdote Sample

My Friends

My friends are EXTREMELY cool because they are my friends. My friends are not ordinary, they're the opposite of ordinary because they're there when I need them. *When my Grandma died, my two best friends, Anna and Haley, came over and spent the night with me to keep me company. They listened to me tell stories about my Grandma and we even laughed a little. Anna said I was really lucky to have a Grandma a Gran like that.* They keep me from doing stuff I might regret later in life. Friends are friendly people you should be able to keep secrets with. Friends make me laugh and keep me from getting bored. Friends are people you can trust, who won't hurt you or take your things. Friends make you laugh when you're down and feeling blue. Friends can tell when you're sad so you can't hide your feelings from your friends. Friends make you smile no matter if it's snowing, raining, or other bad storms. They always make you have a smile. Friends are caring. When you get hurt, they're always there. Helpful, kind, and caring—that's my friends.

Date

Observations

Notes for Future Instruction

Sixth-Grade Student Writing Sample
With General Statements

<u>My Friends</u>

My friends are EXTREMELY cool because they are my friends. My friends are not ordinary, they're the opposite of ordinary because they're there when I need them. They keep me from doing stuff I might regret later in life. Friends are friendly people you should be able to keep secrets with. Friends make me laugh and keep me from getting bored. Friends are people you can trust, who won't hurt you or take your things. Friends make you laugh when you're down and feeling blue. Friends can tell when you're sad so you can't hide your feelings from your friends. Friends make you smile no matter if it's snowing, raining, or other bad storms. They always make you have a smile. Friends are caring. When you get hurt, they're always there. Helpful, kind, and caring—that's my friends.

Tell It in Slow-Mo

Slow motion, or "slow-mo," writing is a technique writers use to slow down the action in order to make it more exciting or suspenseful. In this lesson, students learn how to take an event and slow it down to describe each detail of the action.

Learning Goal: Students will be able to elaborate on a detail in their writing by describing the action in slow motion.

Traits: Ideas, voice, word choice

Introduction: To introduce the concept of slow motion, invite a student to act out an exciting part of a game, such as catching a fly ball or kicking a goal in soccer. Then, have him or her do the same action in slow motion. Talk about the differences between the two actions and why the second is called slow motion, or "slow-mo." Discuss the fact that in slow motion, the viewer sees more of the details of the action. Writers use the same technique to slow down action in a story in order to make it more exciting and let the reader in on more of the details. Read the two examples of throwing a snowball:

- Mallory threw a snowball at her dad as he came around the corner.
- With a sneaky smile, Mallory reached for a handful of soft sticky snow with her right hand. With her left hand, she patted and carefully molded the ball so that it fit just right into her mitten. Squinting from the bright snow, she reached back, aimed, and hurled the snowball forward with all her might. Flying through the air, it seemed to veer a little to the left and almost seemed to stop in midair before hitting its target: right between her dad's shoulder blades!

Have students discuss what makes the second example more effective than the first. The second piece takes the same bit of information and tells it in slow motion, so we can picture the event in our minds. Sometimes slowing down a piece of writing actually makes it more exciting. In this lesson, students will work on the strategy of slowing down a piece of action—what we call slow-mo writing.

Today, you are going to work on describing an interesting or exciting event in slow motion, in other words, taking the reader right into the experience detail by detail. When we do slow-mo writing, we describe the action frame by frame, even second by second. We might describe what the writer is seeing, hearing, touching, tasting, or smelling. We can also tell how the writer is feeling or thinking. We can show facial

Date

Observations

Notes for Future Instruction

NOTES

Date

_____

_____

Observations

_____
_____
_____
_____
_____
_____
_____
_____
_____
_____
_____
_____

Notes for Future Instruction

_____
_____
_____
_____
_____
_____
_____
_____
_____
_____
_____
_____

expressions or even things going on outside the character. We want our reader to be part of the action, so we want to paint as clear a picture as possible.

Instruction: Display the example in Figure 4.9 or create one of your own to demonstrate and think aloud the process of writing in slow-mo. Write as you think aloud about the moment-by-moment details.

This isn't a bad story, I think, but it could use a little work. First, I've listed all the things that have happened, but I haven't really focused on the most exciting part. What do you think is the most exciting part? Let's construct the moment-by-moment details.

Julie and I each gathered up a handful of gravel, then mounted our bikes.

This might be a good time to describe how we looked and felt.

Our faces were grim as we pedaled down the street at breakneck speed, our bottoms raised right off the bicycle seats, one hand on the handlebar and the other filled with pebbles, ready to do battle.

How can we create a visual image that we were going pretty fast?

The houses flew by on either side of the street, just a blur of stucco and siding.

Now we've reached the actual attack. Let's slow it down frame by frame.

As we came toward our tormentors, we slowed down, raised our fists, and bombarded them with gravel.

How are we feeling right now?

In a moment of triumph, we both turned back to check the damage.

FIGURE 4.9. Writing Sample for Slow-Mo Writing

How I Got This Scar

When I was growing up, my cousin and I had a regular feud with a couple of bullies down the street. Every time we rode our bikes past them, they threw stones at us. We had two choices: Give up and go around the block or stay and fight them. We decided to fight. This time, we got ourselves armed with a handful of stones before we headed down the street. As we drove past the bullies, we threw our ammunition.

Unfortunately, as we threw our stones, Julie and I crashed into each other, and I got my foot tangled in the spokes of my bicycle wheel. The good news was that the bullies never bothered us again. The bad news was that I couldn't ride my bike for a week while my sprained toe healed.

How about the collision?

> That's when it happened. Our handlebars collided, sending me flying to the gritty pavement, my bare toes tangled in my bicycle spokes.

Show Figure 4.10, which is a sample of the revised text, and discuss.

Let's talk about what we did here:

1. *We looked for the most exciting or important part and slowed it down to make it more interesting for our reader.*

2. *We told how the characters felt and what they were thinking.*

3. *We painted a mental picture for the reader.*

4. *We described the event frame by frame.*

5. *We used interesting and powerful words.*

Guided Practice: Have each student work with a partner to choose one of the following scenarios and describe it in slow-mo, using techniques for slowing down an interesting or exciting event:

- Falling off a ladder
- Diving into a swimming pool
- Eating a loaded hot dog
- Scoring a goal
- Crossing the finish line

Independent Application: Have students revise a piece of writing to elaborate on an important event using slow-mo writing.

FIGURE 4.10. Slow-Mo Example Revised

How I Got This Scar

Julie and I each gathered up a handful of gravel, then mounted our bikes. Our faces were grim as we pedaled down the street at breakneck speed, our bottoms raised right off the bicycle seats, one hand on the handlebar and the other filled with pebbles, ready to do battle. The houses flew by on either side of the street, just a blur of stucco and siding. As we came toward our tormentors, we slowed down, raised our fists, and bombarded them with gravel. In a moment of triumph, we both turned back to check the damage. That's when it happened. Our handlebars collided, sending me flying to the gritty pavement, my bare toes tangled in my bicycle spokes.

Dabble in Dialogue

Dialogue supports elaboration and idea development in a variety of ways, from defining characters to adding information to the back story. There are many wonderful literary texts that demonstrate effective use of dialogue. Start with a favorite example, then scaffold students' writing to gradually include more effective use of dialogue.

We want our students in grades 4–6 to be able to write interesting and engaging dialogue that enhances the overall text, and we also want them to be able to conquer the accompanying conventions: setting off dialogue with quotation marks, separating a tag line and the talk with punctuation, and starting a new paragraph with each new speaker. It is an ideal opportunity to teach conventions in the context of authentic writing. Depending on your students' prior knowledge about constructing dialogue, this lesson may have to be spread over two days.

Learning Goal: Students will be able to inject dialogue effectively into a piece of writing, using quotation marks and tag lines.

Traits: Ideas, voice, conventions

Introduction: Review previous learning about elaboration techniques before introducing the use of dialogue in writing.

What happens when you've got two or more characters in a story? You want them to talk to each other! We call this "dialogue," a conversation among two or more characters in written text. Today, you're going to learn about how to elaborate on ideas in writing by using dialogue.

Use a sample from a favorite text or the sample below from *Winner!* by Paul Kropp (2008) to show students an example of how writers use small bits of dialogue to add extra information and more voice to the narrative:

> Inside our room, my mom let out a scream. It was something I'd never heard before—a scream of joy.
> "I won!" my mom screamed again. "I won! I won!"
> "Josh, I think I've got a problem here," I told my friend.
> "It sounds like good news to me," he said.
> My mom came rushing out the door. She was holding a lottery ticket in her hand. (pp. 8–9)

Explain to the students that this is an example of dialogue—when two or more characters are talking. Writers use dialogue to add details and voice to writing. Talk about how much more energy it adds to the writing to have the mom shouting than for the author to simply say, "My mom had won the lottery." Tell students that in this lesson, they will be learning how to use dialogue in their writing.

Instruction: For this lesson, you may want to use the sample conversation provided or record a conversation between two of your own students. Jot down what they say—word for word, with every "um," "uh," and repetition—and (with permission) display it for the students. The following includes an example of a conversation I overheard in a classroom and how I used it with the students to teach them about dialogue:

Whenever people are talking to each other, it's called dialogue. Dialogue goes on all the time. I hear dialogue on the playground and in the hallways. In fact, here's a bit of dialogue I heard yesterday when you were coming into the classroom after lunch.

Display the dialogue in Figure 4.11.

This conversation wouldn't be hard to understand if we heard it, but it's pretty hard to read. There are repeated words, pauses, and incomplete thoughts. That's why talking out loud isn't exactly like talking in writing. We want dialogue in writing to sound natural but without all the pauses and repetitions and ums and ahs. After all, it has to be understood by someone who isn't in the room with the speakers.

With the students, use a shared writing approach to rewrite the conversation in Figure 4.11 in "book language," writing each character's words on colored sentence strips. For example, use pink sentence strips for Haley's words and yellow for Janey's.

FIGURE 4.11. Dialogue Sample

Haley: Are those, like, new boots? I love them, like, where did you get those new boots? I just love the color!

Janey: Um...I got...my mom bought them for me in um...um...I think New York when she was, like, traveling there last um...

Haley: I love 'em, love 'em! I want some! Are those the ones called, like...uh...uh...

Janey: Uggs, they're called Uggs, Uggs. What a weird name. And they come in other colors, like, they cost a lot, I know, I think, like purple, turquoise. But, like, my favorite is pink, but they cost a lot. Um, I think $100, I think.

Talk with the students about repetitions, punctuation signals, and unnecessary words (for example, *like*). You might come up with something like the dialogue in Figure 4.12. Read the new dialogue together and talk with the students about why this is easier to read. Does it still convey the message and the characters' voices? Do the students need to make any revisions to the language to remain true to the original conversation?

Next, talk about the differences between their sentence strip dialogue and the sample from *Winner!* or another literary text. In-text dialogue usually has tag lines to tell who is speaking and quotation marks to separate the speaker from the speech.

What do you notice about the dialogue in this section? In writing, we don't have colored strips to separate the different characters' speech, so we have to identify the speaker and the speech in other ways. Can you notice the way that we identify the person who is talking? We call this a <u>tag line</u>. Think about the game of tag. When someone is tagged, we say, "You're it!" Well, the tag line is a way of saying "you're it" in the dialogue. Instead, the writer might use, "she said" or "asked Joe." What are some of the tag lines in this example?

Also, we need to separate the speech from the tag line, so we use quotation marks. Notice how the author frames the talking part with quotation marks, almost like an invisible speech bubble.

FIGURE 4.12. Sentence Strips With Sample Dialogue

> Are those new boots? I just love the color! Where did you get them?

> My mom got them for me in New York when she was there last week.

> I love them, love them, love them! I want some! What are they called, again? I can't remember.

> They're called Uggs. What a weird name! And they come in other colors, like turquoise, but my favorite is pink.

Use a short sentence strip or oversized sticky note to create a tag for each line and experiment with putting the tag in different places in the sentence to see which works best.

Going back to your students' dialogue, look at Haley's first words. Use a different-colored pen to indicate quotation marks around her words. (Some teachers have students glue dried macaroni on the page to represent punctuation marks. A fun idea, perhaps, but I haven't found that it packs enough extra pedagogical punch to be worth the time and effort borrowed from writing time.) Note that this lesson focuses on only one aspect of punctuation at a time.

"Are those new boots? I just love the color! Where did you get them?"

Now, let's add a tag. We might use "Haley said," but I don't think the word <u>said</u> gives enough of an indication of how she said those words. What are some other words we might use instead? Haley cried, shouted, exclaimed, squealed, screamed.... Okay, "Haley squealed" will be our tag line.

Where should the tag line go? Aha! For once, there's no rule! It can go at the beginning of the speech, at the end, or in the middle—whatever sounds best. Let's try the tag line in different places.

Show the students the following examples by moving the tag lines:

- Haley squealed "Are those new boots? I just love the color! Where did you get them?"
- "Are those new boots? I just love the color! Where did you get them?" Haley squealed.
- "Are those new boots?" Haley squealed. "I just love the color! Where did you get them?"

Read each quote aloud together. All are correct, but have the students turn and talk with a partner about which one they think sounds best.

There are still other mechanical issues to deal with: commas to separate the tag lines from the rest of the quotes and starting a new paragraph with each new speaker. You will need to assess the level of understanding of your students to determine an appropriate time to pile on more concepts or leave this to another minilesson. Use excerpts from literature to guide students in constructing generalizations about additional dialogue conventions.

Guided Practice: Have students work in pairs to construct a dialogue between two fictional characters. Use the reproducible provided at the end of this minilesson or bring in two shoes, such as a fancy, high-heeled pump and a ratty, old sneaker. What might the shoes "say" to

Date

Observations

Notes for Future Instruction

Date

_____

Observations

_____
_____
_____
_____
_____
_____
_____
_____
_____
_____
_____

Notes for Future Instruction

_____
_____
_____
_____
_____
_____
_____
_____
_____
_____
_____

each other? Invite each student member of the pairs to take on one of the roles and engage in a short conversation before putting the dialogue in writing. You may want to start by giving them colored sentence strips for generating dialogue or move right to connected text with tag lines and quotation marks.

Independent Application: Invite students to revise a previous draft or a work in progress by inserting short bits of dialogue. An important feature of this minilesson is that students view dialogue as part of a larger piece rather than an end in itself.

Dabble in Dialogue

Work with a partner to create an imaginary conversation between the two shoes. Be sure to add tag lines and quotation marks.

CHAPTER 5

Researching and Writing Informational Texts

It has happened more times than I care to count: I have given my students the assignment to write a report—on a country, a planet, a famous person in history, or various other topics of great interest and relevance—only to be disappointed when they handed in papers that were little more than a collection of snippets copied from Internet sites. Although most of us are pretty diligent about taking students through a multistep writing process for narratives and stories, when it comes to expository writing in subject areas outside of the language arts, process often seems to fly out the window.

It's no wonder that so many of our students view research writing as little more than an exercise in cutting and pasting when they have no other tools in their toolboxes. The research report is a ubiquitous assignment in intermediate classrooms—and for good reason. Research enables our students to delve deeper into topics of their own interest. *Writing Next*, the report of the Carnegie Corporation of New York, cited "inquiry activities" as one of the 11 elements of writing instruction that have a positive impact on adolescent writing (Graham & Perin, 2007). When students engage in inquiry and research projects, they read, they write, and they analyze, critique, and transform information.

Informational writing structures help students organize their thinking in ways that are different from narrative story structures. The ability to gather and analyze information and then present that information in a clear and interesting way to readers is a skill that is essential through school and throughout life.

There are few places where the symbiotic relationship between reading and writing strategies is more evident than in accessing informational text. Students must read text to gather information for writing. They need to sift and sort information to select that which is relevant to their purposes. They must learn the unique structures of informational text, negotiating not just the print but also the visuals, such as pictures, charts, tables, and graphs. Both reading and writing require students to learn to use organizers, such as tables of contents, indexes, and glossaries. Even as students create informational text, they are improving their ability to read it.

The research report must be taught, just like any other text form. Whether the writing task is part of a science, social studies, visual arts, or language arts class, students need explicit instruction in how to gather information and present it in a coherent and well-crafted written form.

The seven minilessons in this chapter offer a teaching sequence for taking a piece of informational writing from planning to publication, as described in the following section. In this chapter, I have taken the same demonstration piece of writing on "The Story of Chocolate" (see the reproducible following Telegram Notes on page 96) through these steps, from gathering information to revising for sentence fluency and word choice—along with examples of "teacher talk" that I might use in presenting the minilessons to students (see Table 5.1 for an overview of the minilessons in this chapter).

When I teach this unit, I reproduce a copy of the first draft on an interactive white board, overhead transparency, or flip chart, and demonstrate all revisions on the same piece, in the same way that I encourage intermediate students to complete all their revisions on the same draft. Conversely, when using this text for student practice in revision, I generally make clean copies of the draft each time. Obviously, the lesson structures will work just as well if you choose to create your own demonstration texts.

TABLE 5.1. Researching and Writing Informational Reports at a Glance

Minilesson	Page	Trait(s) Addressed	Lesson Focus
Thick and Thin Questions	88	Ideas	Planning research questions
Telegram Notes	92	Ideas	Researching with jot notes
Terrific Topic Sentences	97	Ideas, organization	Paragraphing with topic sentences
Bookend Paragraphs	100	Ideas, organization, voice	Writing effective opening and closing paragraphs
Add Some Bling!	104	Ideas, voice, word choice, sentence fluency	Techniques for adding voice and interest to informational writing
The First Four Words: Making Your Sentences Flow	107	Word choice, sentence fluency	Revising sentence beginnings for fluency and variety
Replacing Repeated Words	110	Word choice, sentence fluency	Revising to replace duplicated words and phrases

Many of the minilessons in this chapter introduce fairly complex strategies, such as taking notes, developing research questions, and writing topic sentences, any of which may require more attention than one brief minilesson. As always, assessment of student progress should guide the pacing, presentation, and lesson sequence.

1. *Analyze writing samples of the text form.* When teaching a unit on any genre or text form, I always start by providing students with opportunities to read and analyze both published and student examples of the form. In fact, in our book *The Write Genre: Classroom Activities and Mini-Lessons That Promote Writing With Clarity, Style and Flashes of Brilliance* (Rog & Kropp, 2004), Paul Kropp and I recommend "immersing" students in the genre to ensure that they understand the structure of the texts they are about to write. There are many examples of good informational writing for intermediate students, from magazines, such as *National Geographic Kids*, *Owl*, and *Time for Kids*, to picture books by Seymour Simon, Linda Granfield, Sneed B. Collard III, Gail Gibbons, and others.

Student writing can also be a powerful example for peers. For example, you may want to share the sixth-grade report on ancient Egypt in Figure 5.1.

FIGURE 5.1. Sixth Grader's Research Report on Ancient Egypt

Ancient Egypt

The life of an average child in ancient Egypt was very different from modern life. They had schools, pets and homes, but they were a lot different. There was a smaller variety of pets, but some were very unusual. Childhood did not last as long as it does today.

Egyptian childhood was nothing like modern childhood. If you were an Egyptian child, you'd be running around without clothes on most of the time! And what about hairdos? Boys had a plait that was on the right side of their heads and the rest of the head was shaved.

School was also harder. Children went to school at a young age. But if you were a girl, at age 12 you would have to stay home. Students used either plastered board or stone to write on (just like on the Flintstones). If a child was not listening, they might be beaten.

Animals played a part in ancient Egyptian life. Your family pet was probably a dog, cat or monkey. To show their love for their cat, people would shave off their eyebrows when it died!

If you were an ancient Egyptian, you would eat mostly vegetables. Richer people enjoyed beef and poultry, especially goose. But people thought that fish and pork were not clean.

As you can see, the life of an Egyptian child was quite interesting, but I think I would rather live today.

Invite the students to discuss what makes it a good piece of informational text with guiding questions, such as the following:

- What do you notice about the topic and details? (unusual and interesting details, focused topic, not too broad, topic that is something the writer is interested in)

- What do you notice about how the paragraphs are organized? (all details on the same subtopic together, first [topic] sentence in each paragraph prepares the reader for the information to follow)

- What do you notice about the beginning and ending? (opening gives an overview of the topic, ending reviews and offers a personal statement)

- What do you notice about the personality and style of the piece? What techniques did the writer use to add voice to this piece? (friendly tone, questions, exclamations, parenthetical comment, use of "I" and "you")

As the students delve into examples of the genre, we construct a framework, usually around the six traits, so students have a clear understanding of the characteristics of the form. A framework for informational writing might look like this:

Ideas	Organization	Voice	Word Choice	Sentence Fluency	Conventions
• A topic is developed with factual details.	• The opening introduces the topic. • Details are clustered by subtopic. • Paragraphs usually have topic sentences.	• The writing speaks to a reader through an interesting and engaging tone.	• There may be technical words, specific to the topic. • Most vocabulary is specific and precise rather than flowery.	• Sentences flow smoothly and sound good read aloud.	• Accurate spelling, punctuation, capitalization, and grammar make the writing easy to read.

2. *Choose a topic and narrow it down.* Once students have a clear understanding of what makes a good piece of informational writing, they can begin the prewriting stage of their own masterpieces. The first step is topic selection. You may want to link this writing unit to a theme in science or social studies, requiring students to align their writing topics or research questions with content studies. For example, in a science unit on space, you might brainstorm a range of topics such as "Should Pluto be a planet?" and "Could there be life on Mars?" One of the most important aspects of an effective inquiry project is student choice. Let students choose topics that they are interested in, know about, or want to know more about.

A common problem for intermediate writers is selecting topics that are too broad. We want to teach students to "skinny down" their topics to a manageable size—one that not only offers scope for research but also limits the length of the piece. As with all other text forms, I want my students' writing to be long enough to express the key ideas but short enough to maintain quality. Two or three hundred words (about two handwritten pages) are enough for an intermediate-grade report.

3. *Create a list of possible research questions.* We know that good writing is focused. One problem for writers of all ages is rambling on with a collection of random facts that are only loosely tied together. Sometimes the research piece is so bloated with irrelevant information that it's hard to figure out what point the writer is trying to make. Many young writers have trouble distinguishing what's important from what's merely interesting (Harvey & Goudvis, 2007). Starting with three or four key research questions or subtopics related to the main topic helps writers focus their research and keeps the writing to a length manageable enough to sustain quality and encourage revision.

The challenge of research questions is to make them "thick" enough. In other words, we're looking for the Goldilocks principle: not too big, not too small, but "just right." For intermediate students, I like to define a "just right" question as one that can generally be addressed in a paragraph of four to six facts or details. Determining research questions can be the hardest part of the process for some writers. **Thick and Thin Questions** invites students to brainstorm a list of possible questions that they might include in their research. After doing some general reading about the question, the students prune their question list by combining thin questions, breaking down thick questions, and deleting questions that won't fit into this research. They might even add a new question or two that emerged from the reading.

4. *Gather information on the topic.* How do you get students to take adequate notes without plagiarizing large chunks of text? I like to draw an analogy to good old-fashioned telegrams, in which every word costs money! **Telegram Notes** provides modeling and practice in selecting the key words the students will record. The "gathering grid" (see the reproducible following Thick and Thin Questions on page 91) is a graphic organizer for collecting information on a topic. In each of the boxes in the first column, the student writes one of the research questions or topics. In each of the boxes across the top row, the student writes the name and bibliographic information about the source of the information. The student will then use the boxes below the source heads to gather information about each question from each source.

You'll need to decide what bibliographic information you want students to include and teach them to record that information. For intermediate students, I find it sufficient to record the author, title, and publication date (or URL and download date). I generally require the students to use at least three sources, only one of which can be an Internet site. As they research, they write notes on the section of the grid that corresponds to each question and source. Reproducing the gathering grid on 11" × 17" paper allows a little more space for writing, while still limiting the amount of text that can fit into the box.

5. *Transfer the notes into a first draft with sentences and paragraphs.*
Once students have accumulated enough information in their gathering grids, they are ready to transform their telegram notes into connected text: the first draft. The great advantage to the gathering grid is that it organizes the information in advance. Usually, the notes for each research question or topic will form one paragraph; next, the writer needs focus on crafting the notes into sentences.

Even when the content is all in place in the gathering grid, however, many intermediate students will have trouble transforming their notes into connected text. Although it was beyond the scope of this book to include minilessons on drafting, I urge teachers to use one or more minilessons to model and think aloud the process of creating well-crafted sentences and coherent paragraphs form the information in the telegram notes.

As we demonstrate how to compose a draft, we also want to guide students in using a tone that speaks to a reader and conveys the information in an interesting and engaging style. We used to think that informational text should be direct, matter-of-fact, and without voice. Our thinking has changed in today's world, where most informational text is every bit as rich and engaging as narrative text (and often reads like narrative text). We want our students' writing to sound more like today's *National Geographic* and less like the encyclopedias of old.

The one thing we don't want to encourage is the ubiquitous "hamburger paragraph," commonly described as a topic sentence, three details, and a wrap-up sentence. Let's face it, some paragraphs will have two details, while others will have 20; it just depends on the writer, the topic, and the text! And as far as topic sentences are concerned, they usually appear at the beginning of a paragraph and occasionally may appear at the end or buried in the middle, but they are never repeated at the beginning *and* the end of the paragraph in any kind of authentic writing.

I spent a long time considering whether to include a minilesson on topic sentences in this chapter. After all, in Richard Braddock's (1975) classic study, he found that only about 13% of expository paragraphs opened with explicit topic statements—and cautioned teachers and textbooks not to teach them. More

> ### Teaching Sequence for Informational Writing
>
> 1. Analyze writing samples of the text form.
> 2. Choose a topic and narrow it down.
> 3. Create a list of possible research questions.
> 4. Gather information on the topic.
> 5. Transfer the notes into a first draft with sentences and paragraphs.
> 6. Add introductory and concluding paragraphs.
> 7. Revise for voice, word choice, and sentence fluency.
> 8. Polish and publish.

recent research has questioned Braddock's findings (Smith, 2008), and there is general agreement that the topic sentence is a useful structure for helping developing writers organize their thinking and their writing. Therefore, I decided to include the minilesson **Terrific Topic Sentences**, which teaches students to create topic sentences for informational paragraphs, using a literature link, and helps reinforce the connection between reading and writing. When students learn to look for the topic sentence in informational text, it helps them define the main idea and supporting details in what they read as well as what they write.

6. *Add introductory and concluding paragraphs.* I usually encourage students to draft the body of the piece first and then add the introductory and concluding paragraphs. **Bookend Paragraphs** teaches students to generate introductory paragraphs that grab the reader's attention and concluding paragraphs that provide a satisfying culmination to the piece.

7. *Revise for voice, word choice, and sentence fluency.* Once students have a draft in place, it's time to *re-view* and revise the text for writer's craft. **Add Some Bling!** offers a range of writers' techniques to help students add voice to their writing. This minilesson uses a constructivist approach, inviting students to search for writers' techniques, then categorize and label them. This approach is useful for many different lessons, from similes to vivid verbs. As students build a repertoire of writing "bling," they can use these crafting techniques in initial drafting or insert them later in the revision process.

The final two minilessons in this chapter focus on word choice and sentence fluency. **The First Four Words: Making Your Sentences Flow** helps writers attend to the flow and rhythm of the text by revising sentence beginnings. **Replacing Repeated Words** reminds writers to spice up their writing by exchanging duplicated words and phrases for more interesting synonyms.

8. *Polish and publish.* Of course, before any piece of writing is taken to publication, we must get out that editing cloth and polish up the conventions. A simple process for self-editing may be found on page 193. You will want to build minilessons on spelling patterns, punctuation, capitalization, subject–verb agreement, and the like into this unit. Use your local curriculum and your own assessments of your students' strengths and weaknesses to determine which lessons are appropriate at this point.

Research writing offers many interesting opportunities for publication. This is a good time to teach students about word processing, presentation of their work, adding visuals, and including a bibliography and other text features. We want our students to build long-term strategies for choosing topics of interest, collecting data, and sharing what they've learned in text that is interesting and engaging for a reader. Carefully planned lessons that demonstrate the processes of informational writing are the best antidote for pirated papers and tired text.

NOTES

Date

_____

Observations

_____
_____
_____
_____
_____
_____
_____
_____
_____
_____
_____

Notes for Future Instruction

_____
_____
_____
_____
_____
_____
_____
_____
_____
_____
_____

Thick and Thin Questions

Good writing is focused. It sticks to one topic and develops that topic with rich and interesting details. Starting with three or four key research questions or subtopics related to the main topic helps writers focus their research and their writing as a whole. The challenge of research questions is to make them "thick" enough. If the question is too "thin," it can be fully answered in just a sentence or two. Students should choose research questions that are thick enough to generate a paragraph of information. This minilesson is just an introduction to the process of developing a set of appropriate research questions on a chosen topic. Depending on the proficiency and background of your students, you may want to allow more time for reading and researching. To keep the research paper focused and manageable, I usually have students focus on three to five research questions. We add "What are some other interesting facts?" which opens the door to additional ideas and details that might enrich the final piece.

Learning Goal: Students will be able to generate three to five appropriate research questions on a topic of their choice.

Trait: Ideas

Introduction: Remind the students that selecting a topic is only the first step in planning a research paper. They also have to think about what they would like to know about that topic. Choosing three to five big idea questions to research helps writers focus their research and makes the final paper easier to write.

We've been looking at a lot of examples of informational writing, and we've all been thinking about what topics we'd like to research. Once I've chosen a topic, then I need to think about what I want to learn about that topic and what I want my readers to know. That's why my next step is to make a list of questions or subtopics that I want to tackle. Some topics are too thin; there's just not a lot of information about them. Today you're going to learn about creating nice, thick research questions about your topic.

Instruction: Think aloud for the students as you share a broad topic and some specific research questions.

I have decided that I'm going to do some research on one of my favorite topics: chocolate! But before I can begin to write, I need to decide what I want to find out

about chocolate. I already know a thing or two about it, and I've started to do a little research, so I have a few ideas of questions I might like to include.

You might provide a list of questions or have the students help you generate a list, as in Figure 5.2.

Have students turn and talk about why some of these questions are better than others. A question like "Who invented chocolate?" might be interesting, but it's also kind of thin. It could be answered in one sentence—or even one word. A good question should have enough details to fill about a paragraph of writing. Talk about how a thicker question could include several subquestions. For example, a question like "How was chocolate invented?" would probably include the answer to "Who invented chocolate?" "How is chocolate made?" would likely incorporate "How is white chocolate different from brown?" and other facts as well.

Think aloud as you choose three to five thick questions from the list. Remind students that it is often necessary to do some research about the topic before writers can come up with the best questions.

So, out of that nice long list that you helped me create, I've chosen these thick questions:

- *How is chocolate made?*

- *How was chocolate invented?*

- *What is chocolate used for?*

Plus, I added this one: What are some other interesting facts?

FIGURE 5.2. Possible Research Questions for Chocolate

- How is chocolate made?
- Who invented chocolate?
- What is chocolate used for?
- Where does chocolate come from?
- (How) was chocolate invented?
- Why do so many people love chocolate?
- Why do some people hate chocolate?
- How many kinds of chocolate are there?
- How is white chocolate different from brown?
- What can you make out of chocolate?
- How do you make chocolate candies?

NOTES

Date

_____

Observations

_____
_____
_____
_____
_____
_____
_____
_____
_____

Notes for Future Instruction

_____
_____
_____
_____
_____
_____
_____
_____
_____
_____

Reproduce a copy of a blank gathering grid and model for the students how to write the questions into the boxes in the first column of the grid. (A reproducible gathering grid can be found at the end of this minilesson.) The top row allows space to record the title and bibliographical information about different sources that are used. The remaining boxes are used for gathering notes on the topic.

Guided Practice: Choose a topic that is familiar to the students, such as a recent area of study in science or social studies. As a group, brainstorm a list of possible research questions on that topic. Have students work with a partner to sort thick questions from thin ones and discuss which questions they would use if they were to research this topic.

Independent Application: Students should begin to brainstorm lists of questions for their own research topic. Allow time for them to read and research before choosing their final three to five key questions for their gathering grids. Offer support in topic selection. If students can't come up with a list of thick questions, it could be that the topic was not the best choice. Share the reproducible gathering grid and, if possible, enlarge the student copies to 11" × 17" to provide adequate writing space. Have the students write their thick questions in the first column.

Gathering Grid

Research Questions	Source 1:	Source 2:	Source 3:

Telegram Notes

Avoiding plagiarism can be difficult for intermediate writers. One way to prevent students from copying directly from sources is to teach them how to take point-form notes. I find that it helps to make an analogy to old-fashioned telegrams, in which every word costs money. The challenge for writers is to keep the notes brief but still write enough to remember what the fact was about. To use the gathering grid for telegram note-taking, list the research questions in the left column and the resources across the top. Each column is used to collect notes from that particular resource.

Learning Goal: Students will be able to gather research by taking point-form notes.

Trait: Ideas

Introduction: Make a connection to previous work on topics and research questions in informational writing. Explain to students the importance of gathering information about a topic without copying from another source. Tell them that they will be practicing writing brief bits of information that are just long enough to get the gist of the idea, kind of like old-fashioned telegrams.

Now that we have our research questions, we need to start gathering answers from books and other sources. However, we can't just copy every word right from the Internet or another book or article. That's not fair to the people who did the writing—and, in fact, it's against the law! We can, however, pull the important facts out of the writing and then rewrite those facts in our own words.

So, how can we choose the important parts without copying the whole thing? Well, let's think about the olden days, long before e-mail and texting. If you wanted to get a message to someone in a big hurry, your only choice was to send them a telegram. The problem with telegrams, though, was that they were expensive. Every word cost money, so you didn't want to use any words that weren't necessary. I like to think of gathering information from books as making "telegram notes." If every word costs money, which words could you leave out and still keep all of the meaning? Today, you're going to practice using telegram notes to gather information about a topic.

Instruction: Find a short piece of informational text or display the student piece "A World of Chocolate" that follows this minilesson. Make a copy of the gathering grid on page 91 and demonstrate how to use it to record the author, title, publication date, and any other bibliographical information you want students to include. Think aloud as you read through the text sentence by sentence, considering whether the information in the sentence fits with any of our research questions. We talk about whether the information in the sentence is important (in other words, does it answer any of our questions?) or just interesting (not relevant to our note-taking). Then, model for the students how to use telegram notes to record the information on the grid.

Let's look at the first sentence: "Can you believe that 500 years ago, no one had heard of chocolate?" That's pretty interesting, and it makes me want to read on, but it doesn't really give us any information to answer our questions. "Before that, people only had cocoa, which is a powder made from beans that grow on a tree called a cacao." This fits right into our question about how chocolate is made. How can I record that information without using too many words? Let's try "cocoa powder from cacao tree beans."

"It wasn't until the 1500s that people in Europe learned how to turn cocoa into chocolate." Now we're getting somewhere! This could be answering two of my questions: "How is chocolate made?" and "How was chocolate invented?" Remember the telegram principle: Every word costs money. How can I put down this fact using as few words as possible? I'm just going to write: "1500s—Europe—turned cocoa to chocolate." Is that enough? I think so!

Read the next sentence: "They roasted and crushed the cocoa beans." What's this telling us? It answers our question "How is chocolate made?" I'm going to write, "roasted and crushed cocoa beans." When we write telegram notes, we don't need little words like <u>they</u>, <u>the</u>, and <u>a</u>. Instead, we often use dashes or dots to join random words in an idea.

Your turn! Read the last sentence in the paragraph: "Then, they mixed the beans with sugar and water to make liquid chocolate to drink." Is that important or just interesting? Which question does it answer? Turn and talk to your neighbor about what words you would use to write this telegram note.

Cover the text and have students look only at the notes taken so far. Your notes may look something like the example in Figure 5.3. Have them turn and talk about what they remember about the information in the first part of the report, using only the notes. Invite discussion about whether the notes were adequate for recalling information. Would they be adequate for recalling information in a week or a month? If not, talk about what information they might need to add, change, or delete to make the notes more useful.

NOTES

Date

Observations

Notes for Future Instruction

FIGURE 5.3. Sample Gathering Grid for "A World of Chocolate"

Research Questions	Source 1: "A World of Chocolate" by Alex	Source 2: The Story of Chocolate by Carolyn Jenner ©2005	Source 3:
How is chocolate made?	Beans are roasted, crushed, mixed with sugar + water. Milk chocolate = add butter + milk	-cocoa/cacao beans - seeds of cacao tree -need hot, wet climate (Central and S. America) -1 tree = 2 lbs dried beans	
How was chocolate invented?	1500's - Europeans Chocolate from Cocoa. 1875 - Switzerland 1st milk chocolate	Columbus - first European? 1765 - first American chocolate factory 1875 - first milk chocolate	
What is chocolate used for?	- drinking - baking cocoa		
What are some other interesting facts about chocolate?	- Cocoa beans taste bitter	scientific name - "theobrama" - "food of the gods." Average person - 11 lbs/year (100 candy bars)	

Guided Practice: Have students work with a partner to complete the note-taking for the remainder of this piece of text, using their own copies of a blank gathering grid. You may want to offer more guided practice with telegram note-taking from other pieces of text before sending your students off on their own. Monitor their work and assess their mastery. It's worth taking all the time needed to ensure that students understand the process of note-taking. This will be an important skill in many contexts in years to come and will help them avoid plagiarism as they embark on research writing throughout the rest of their school lives.

Independent Application: Revisit and reflect on the usefulness of the gathering grid. Students should already have gathering grids with their research questions in place. Have them begin note-taking on their own chosen research topics.

Remind students that the remaining boxes in the top row are intended for other sources of information and establish your requirements for acceptable resources. How many different sources should students use? How many Internet sources are acceptable? What other sources do students have at their disposal? It may be necessary to spend some time exploring different types of resources.

Date

Observations

Notes for Future Instruction

A Student's Informational Text on Chocolate

<u>A World of Chocolate</u>
By Alex

Can you believe that 500 years ago, no one had heard of chocolate? Before that, people only had cocoa, which is a powder made from beans that grow on a tree called a cacao. But cocoa beans do not taste good by themselves. They are bitter and turn your mouth brown.

It wasn't until the 1500s that people in Europe learned how to turn cocoa into chocolate. They roasted and crushed the cocoa beans. Then, they mixed the beans with sugar and water to make liquid chocolate to drink.

In 1875, people in Switzerland tried to add butter and milk to liquid chocolate. This was the first milk chocolate. Now it's the world's favorite flavor.

Today, chocolate comes in many different forms. There is hot cocoa to drink. There is powdered chocolate for baking. There is milk chocolate for candy bars. Every day, all over the world, people are enjoying the world's favorite flavor.

Terrific Topic Sentences

A topic sentence introduces and encapsulates the information in the ensuing paragraph. The topic sentence may appear anywhere in the paragraph, but it is most commonly the first sentence. The point made in the topic sentence is developed and supported by the rest of the paragraph. Often, topic sentences smooth the transition from one paragraph to the next. They not only help the reader but also help the writer think about the organization of details and the overall structure of the text.

This lesson uses a literature link and helps reinforce the connection between reading and writing. When students learn to look for the topic sentence in informational text, it helps them define the main idea and supporting details in what they read as well as what they write.

Learning Goal: Students will be able to create topic sentences for informational paragraphs.

Traits: Ideas, organization

Introduction: Read one of the picture books by Sneed B. Collard III, such as *Beaks!* (2002), *Animal Dads* (1997), or *Teeth* (2008). Draw students' attention to the short sentences in bold print at the top of each page and the first sentence in each paragraph. Have them turn and talk about the purpose of these sentences. Students should be able to determine that these sentences give general information about what the rest of the information on the page is going to be about. Tell them that these general statements are called *topic sentences* and are the organizer sentences for every paragraph in informational writing. The topic sentence gives the reader a hint of what the rest of the paragraph will be about.

Instruction: Provide a gathering grid of your own or invite students to look at the sample gathering grid on chocolate (see Figure 5.3 on page 94). For each research question, demonstrate or collaboratively create a topic sentence that introduces the rest of the information.

Let's say that each of my research questions is going to represent one paragraph in my draft. Just to get my thinking organized, I'm going to create a topic sentence for each of my research questions. For example, for "How is chocolate made?" I might write, "All types of chocolate start out as beans from a tree called cacao." The phrase "start out" suggests that I'm going to tell more about how different types of chocolate are made and what happens next.

Date

_____

Observations

_____
_____
_____
_____
_____
_____
_____
_____
_____

Notes for Future Instruction

_____
_____
_____
_____
_____
_____
_____
_____
_____
_____

In the section on how chocolate was discovered, I've got some information about Christopher Columbus, the Spanish, and the ancient Aztecs. I'm going to try to combine those two pieces of information in my topic sentence: "Until 500 years ago, only a few people in the world had ever tasted chocolate."

Guided Practice: Provide pairs or small groups of students with a copy of the reproducible found at the end of this minilesson. Have them work together to create a topic sentence for each paragraph. Use this guided writing activity to assess students' understanding of the concept of topic sentences and to guide future instruction.

Independent Application: Have students revisit their own gathering grids and write a topic sentence for each question or subtopic. They may change their topic sentences as they draft or revise, but the grid gives them an organizer to get started.

Terrific Topic Sentences

Create a topic sentence for each of the following paragraphs:

_____

_____

I don't know which part I like the most: the kids in scary costumes, the carved pumpkins, or the candy, candy, candy! Every year, I plan for months about what I'm going to dress up as, and I usually change my mind at least six times before the big day. My friends and I dash from door to door with our big sacks, filling them with treats until they're almost too heavy to carry. Sometimes, we even play a trick or two, but it's all in fun.

_____

_____

Frogs are characterized by bulging eyes, smooth or slimy skin, and strong, long, webbed hind feet. They prefer warm, moist environments. Toads, however, have dry, warty skin and stubby bodies with short hind legs. That's because toads move by walking, instead of hopping as frogs do.

_____

_____

You should always swim with a buddy. Then, if one of you gets tired or gets in trouble in the water, the other can get help. Swim in safe areas and places that you know. If you can, stick to places that have a lifeguard. Make sure the water is deep enough before you dive. Know your limits and look out for one another.

_____

_____

Mozart began to play the harpsichord when he was only 3 years old, and by the age of 5, he had composed his first piece of music. By the age of 6, he had performed concerts for the king and queen of Austria. Before long, he was giving concerts in all the major cities in Europe.

NOTES

Date

_____

_____

Observations

_____

_____

_____

_____

_____

_____

_____

_____

_____

_____

Notes for Future Instruction

_____

_____

_____

_____

_____

_____

_____

_____

_____

_____

_____

Bookend Paragraphs

This minilesson focuses on teaching students to write introductory and concluding paragraphs, the "bookends" at each end of the body of information. The opening paragraph should grab the reader's attention and introduce the topic. The closing paragraph summarizes the main point and wraps up the piece. Many writers find it easier to write the body of the piece first and then write the introduction and conclusion after most of the content is in place. We often use bling in our introductions and conclusions, so I sometimes teach the minilesson **Add Some Bling!** before **Bookend Paragraphs**.

Learning Goal: Students will be able to craft strong opening and closing paragraphs for a research piece.

Traits: Ideas, organization, voice

Introduction: The students have already been working on putting information into paragraphs. This lesson focuses on the special paragraphs at the beginning and end of the piece. Bring in a set of bookends to demonstrate how bookends go at the front and back of a set of books to hold the collection together. Tell students that the opening and closing paragraphs of a piece of text are kind of like bookends, because they mark the beginning and ending and hold the piece of text together. Today, they are going to read some great bookend paragraphs and practice writing some themselves.

Instruction: Read or display these paragraphs from "A Real-Life Superman" by Rachel Smith (2009). Tell the students that these are the opening and closing paragraphs of an article about basketball star Dwight Howard of the Orlando Magic.

> Scoring from the free-throw line and making impressive dunks on the basketball court are just part of the job for NBA star Dwight Howard, of the Orlando Magic. In the 2008–2009 season, Howard averaged 14 rebounds and 21 points per game.
>
> With stats like that, anyone can see why Howard has been nicknamed "Superman." But during the off-season, Howard shows that he's not only a hero on the court, but off of it too. The center finds time to give back, both at home and across the world. (paras. 1–2)

> Howard is at the height of his career and basketball is the biggest thing on his plate. But however busy he may be, the NBA star still finds time to give back, whether it's through Basketball Without Borders or his own basketball camp for kids. Howard truly is a Superman. (para. 9)

Invite students to talk about the techniques this writer has used to open and close the piece of writing. For example, she grabs our attention with basketball statistics and then introduces the rest of the topic. From the introduction, we know that in the remainder of the piece, we're probably going to read about basketball star Dwight Howard's good works. In the closing paragraph, she reviews the main theme of the piece—basketball as well as charitable works—and circles back to the introduction with a reference to Superman.

Review with the students that effective bookend paragraphs frame the piece of writing by hooking the reader's attention and introducing the topic, then revisiting a key idea and wrapping the piece up neatly.

Use the writing sample on chocolate to demonstrate building bookend paragraphs. Together with the students, build an opening hook and an overview of what the paper is to be about. Then, create a summary of key points and a closing sentence. Think aloud as you compose the opening and closing paragraphs. A reproducible draft of the writing sample on chocolate with completed bookend paragraphs follows this minilesson.

Just like in Rachel Smith's article on Dwight Howard, I need to create an opening paragraph for my piece on chocolate that does two things: grab my reader's attention and tell my reader what the rest of the piece is going to be about. Often, a question is a great way to start a piece. Maybe I'll try this: "What's the world's favorite flavor? If you guessed chocolate, you're right." That will get my reader involved in the piece right off the bat. Then, I need to give a hint about what the rest of the piece is about. I'm going to talk about the history of chocolate and how it's made, so I think I'll say, "From a tree in the rain forests of South America to the chocolate sauce on your ice cream, the story of chocolate is a fascinating one." That not only gives an overview of the piece but also sets the reader up to know that he or she is going to read something very interesting.

We noticed that Rachel Smith ended by reminding us of the key points of the article: Dwight Howard's work helping kids. Then, she used a technique that writers use all the time—a key word from the first paragraph ("Superman") again at the end. We call that a "wraparound" ending. I think I might wrap around to my opening idea on the world's favorite flavor.

As students work on creating opening and closing paragraphs for their writing, some may need additional support. You may want to provide students with some possible sentence stems for a general statement, as in Figure 5.4. Complete the same process with the concluding paragraph. The ending paragraph usually has two parts: It

Date

Observations

Notes for Future Instruction

FIGURE 5.4. Sample Sentence Stems for Bookend Paragraphs

Ways to start a piece of writing:
- It's hard to believe that…
- You'll soon discover that…
- There are many reasons that…
- You may be surprised to learn that…
- It's interesting that…
- Let's take a look at…
- Here is the story of…

Ways to end a piece of writing:
- As you can see, …
- Wouldn't you agree that…
- It's clear that…
- All in all, …

FIGURE 5.5. A Student's Informational Text on Penguins

Penguins live in the southern hemisphere. About ten percent of penguins live in Antarctica, the coldest place in the world.

Penguins can't fly but they can move in other ways. Instead of wings, they have flippers that help them swim. On land, the penguins use their tails and flippers to help them balance. Penguins either waddle on their feet or slide on their bellies across the snow. This is called "tobogganing."

The female penguin lays the egg, then she goes off to find food for the baby. The male takes care of the egg while she is gone. The male holds the egg on his feet and tucks it under his feathers to keep it warm until it hatches. When the female comes back, they take turns looking after the chick.

summarizes or reviews the main points of the piece and then wraps up with a satisfying ending. Again, it might be helpful to offer some sentence stems, as in Figure 5.4.

Guided Practice: Use the sample of informational text on penguins in Figure 5.5 for students to work in groups to create opening and closing paragraphs.

It's always a good activity to send students on a hunt for examples of good bookend paragraphs in books and magazines. Have students write their examples on large sheets of paper and display them for others to read.

Independent Application: Have students work on opening and closing paragraphs for their own research writing piece.

Sample Text: The Story of Chocolate

The Story of Chocolate

What's the world's favorite flavor? If you guessed chocolate, you're right. In fact, the average American eats over 11 pounds of chocolate a year! From a tree in the rain forests of South America to the chocolate sauce on your ice cream, the story of chocolate is a fascinating one.

All types of chocolate start out as beans from a tree called a cacao. The cacao beans are shelled, roasted, and crushed to make cocoa butter. The butter is then heated to make a thick paste called chocolate liquor. Dark chocolate is made with chocolate liquor, cocoa butter, and vanilla. Milk chocolate is made from chocolate liquor, cocoa butter, sugar, and milk. White chocolate is made from just cocoa butter with sugar and milk.

Five hundred years ago, most of the world had never tasted chocolate. In the 1500s, the Aztecs of Central America gave Christopher Columbus a spicy drink made of crushed cacao beans boiled with spices and chili peppers. Columbus brought the chocolate drink back to Spain, where they added sugar instead of peppers. At that time, cacao beans were very hard to get, and chocolate was much too expensive for most people. But by the 1600s, chocolate houses had opened up all over Europe, and drinking chocolate became a popular pastime.

Do you like chocolate bars? In 1847, the first chocolate bars were created by J.S. Fry Company in England, but they tasted bitter and weren't too popular. In 1875, the Swiss figured out how to make milk chocolate by adding milk and sugar to chocolate liquor. In the 1890s, American chocolate manufacturer Milton Hershey made the first milk chocolate bar.

Chocolate has come a long way from its beginnings as a spicy drink. Today, there are over 30,000 kinds of chocolate candies to satisfy your sweet tooth. And if that's not enough, there is even chocolate toothpaste, chocolate pasta, and chocolate soap! No wonder it's the world's favorite flavor!

Marvelous Minilessons for Teaching Intermediate Writing, Grades 4–6 by Lori Jamison Rog. © 2011 International Reading Association.
May be copied for classroom use.

Add Some Bling!

There was a time when we thought informational text should read like the dictionary: dull, flat, and anonymous. Now we know that informational writing, like all writing, should have a flair and style that speaks to a reader. Open an issue of *National Geographic*, *Sports Illustrated*, or almost any other magazine, and you'll see lively informational writing that sparkles with style and voice, as well as interesting content to capture the reader's attention. Amazing facts, quotes, questions, comparisons, and anecdotes are just some of the bling that writers use to make their writing shine.

This minilesson asks students to search print resources for words, phrases, sentences, and ideas that add voice and bling to text. You may choose to spread this lesson out over two or more days, using the first day to identify bling in a read-aloud and the second day for a bling-hunting mission to find samples of voice in other published nonfiction writing.

Learning Goal: Students will be able to identify and apply a range of writers' techniques to add voice and style to informational writing.

Traits: Ideas, voice, word choice, sentence fluency

Introduction: I like to introduce this minilesson by showing the students a sparkly rhinestone brooch that I wear to jazz up my plain, black jacket. Sometimes, we refer to glittering, gold, silver, and jewel-encrusted accessories as bling. And just as people wear bling to add sparkle to their wardrobe, writers of informational text like to add a little bling here and there to make their writing sparkle for a reader. Any technique that makes writing more interesting, engaging, exciting, or unique might be considered writing bling. Tell students that they will be listening for bling in a read-aloud text; then they will have the opportunity to use some of these techniques in their own writing.

Instruction: Read any nonfiction text that sparkles with voice. I like to use picture books like Seymour Simon's (2008) *The Human Body*, drawing students' attention to the techniques the author has used and recording them on an ongoing anchor chart.

Listen to this amazing fact from page 6: "Your body has about 100 trillion cells. That's 100 followed by 12 zeroes!" Why do you think Seymour Simon added that second sentence? He goes on to say, "If you were to count one cell a second nonstop, you would need millions of years to count a single trillion cells!" By adding a couple of amazing facts, he has made us readers part of the text and helped us understand something that is very complex. Amazing facts and comparisons (comparing the information to something the reader can relate to) are just two of the techniques that nonfiction writers use to make their writing more interesting. We might call these techniques bling that make writing sparkle, just as my brooch makes my jacket sparkle. As I read the rest of the book, listen for other bling that the author has used.

During the reading, pause to discuss techniques the writer has used, and record them on a chart. This chart can be an ongoing classroom resource that you add to whenever you and the students discover new techniques. Some of the bling your students point out might include those listed in Figure 5.6.

In subsequent lessons, students will have an opportunity to mine other pieces of literature for bling that makes writing sparkle with voice. Depending on the sophistication of my students, I would probably focus on only a few techniques at a time.

Think aloud as you model adding bling to a piece of writing. Make a copy of "The Story of Chocolate" draft with bookend paragraphs (see page 103) and insert or replace words, phrases, or sentences to add voice and sparkle to the writing.

See if students can identify any bling already in the piece on chocolate. For example, "over 11 pounds of chocolate a year" and "over 30,000 kinds of chocolate candies" are both interesting statistics. Asking a question is another demonstration of bling, as is an exclamation.

Some revisions are illustrated in Figure 5.7, such as the following:

- A fascinating fact or statistic ("It takes 400–500 beans…")

- An interesting comparison ("like gold")

- An example or anecdote ("Milton Hershey noticed children…")

FIGURE 5.6. Examples of Writing Bling

1. A fascinating fact or statistic
2. An interesting comparison
3. A question
4. A connection to the reader
5. A simile or metaphor
6. An exclamation
7. A quote
8. An example or anecdote
9. A touch of humor
10. A personal connection or observation
11. A very short sentence or sentence fragment
12. A colorful description

Date

Observations

Notes for Future Instruction

NOTES

Date

_____

Observations

_____
_____
_____
_____
_____
_____
_____
_____

Notes for Future Instruction

_____
_____
_____
_____
_____
_____
_____
_____
_____

FIGURE 5.7. Text Revised for Bling

The Story of Chocolate

What's the world's favorite flavor? If you guessed chocolate, you're right. In fact, the average American eats over 11 pounds of chocolate a year! From a tree in the rain forests of South America to the chocolate sauce on your ice cream, the story of chocolate is a fascinating one.

All types of chocolate start out as beans from a tree called a cacao. *It takes 400-500 beans to make one pound of chocolate.* The cacao beans are shelled, roasted and crushed to make cocoa butter. The butter is then heated to make a thick paste called chocolate liquor. Dark chocolate is made with chocolate liquor, cocoa butter, and vanilla. Milk chocolate is made from chocolate liquor, cocoa butter, sugar and milk. White chocolate is made from just cocoa butter with sugar and milk.

Five hundred years ago, most of the world had never tasted chocolate. In the 1500s, the Aztecs of Central America gave Christopher Columbus a spicy drink made of crushed cacao beans boiled with spices and peppers. *Although he didn't like the taste of it,* Columbus brought the chocolate drink back to Spain, where they added sugar instead of chilli peppers. At that time, cacao beans were ~~very hard to get~~ *like gold* and chocolate was much too expensive for most people. But by the 1600s, chocolate houses had opened up all over Europe and drinking chocolate became a popular pastime.

Do you like chocolate bars? In 1847, the first chocolate bars were created by the JS Fry Company in England, but they tasted bitter and weren't too popular. In 1875, the Swiss figured out how to make milk chocolate by adding milk and sugar to chocolate liquor. In the 1890s, American chocolate manufacturer Milton Hershey ~~made the first milk chocolate bar.~~

Chocolate has come a long way from its beginnings as a spicy drink. Today there are over 30,000 kinds of chocolate candies to satisfy your sweet tooth. And if that's not enough, there is even chocolate toothpaste, chocolate pasta, and chocolate soap! No wonder it's the world's favorite flavour!

noticed children licking the coating off chocolate-covered caramels — and throwing away the caramels. He decided to make the treat without the caramels — and that was the world's first milk chocolate bar.

Guided Practice: You may want to provide students with a copy of the student writing sample on ancient Egypt (see Figure 5.1 on page 83) that was discussed at the beginning of the chapter and have them work in pairs or small groups to highlight and name some of the bling used in the piece.

Independent Application: Encourage students to add at least two examples of bling to their own drafts.

The First Four Words: Making Your Sentences Flow

One of the problems we sometimes find in informational text is monotonous sentences. Sentence after sentence follows the same subject–verb pattern: "It is…," "They are…," "They have…," and so forth. Instead of keeping the reader interested, this writing practically lulls the reader to sleep! A simple technique for reviving tired writing is to vary the first four words of the sentence. (For a specific sentence variety strategy, see **Flip the Sentence** in Chapter 7.)

Learning Goal: Students will be able to vary the beginnings of sentences in a piece to purposefully create fluency and flow.

Traits: Word choice, sentence fluency

Introduction: Talk with the students about how some writing flows smoothly and other writing sounds choppy.

Let's take a look at my piece on the story of chocolate. I think it's got a pretty strong opener, interesting details, and a satisfying closing. But in some places in the middle, it doesn't really seem to flow. Maybe that's because my sentences are all too much the same. Today, we're going to work on making writing flow more smoothly by varying the beginnings of the sentences.

Instruction: Display the chocolate draft that is in the revision process or make a fresh copy of the draft with bookend paragraphs on page 103. Read the first paragraph aloud to the students and take note of how it seems to flow smoothly to the ear. Highlight or jot down the first four words of each sentence for the students:

- "What's the world's favorite"
- "If you guessed chocolate"
- "In fact, the average"
- "From a tree in"

Notice that the first four words of each sentence in the first paragraph are all different structures. In the first sentence, I started with "what" and asked a question. In the other three sentences, I started with a preposition ("in," "from," "if"). An easy way to give our writing fluency and rhythm is to vary the first four words.

Date

_____

_____

Observations

_____

_____

_____

_____

_____

_____

_____

_____

_____

_____

Notes for Future Instruction

_____

_____

_____

_____

_____

_____

_____

_____

_____

_____

_____

_____

Now, let's look at the first four words of each sentence in the second paragraph:

- *All types of chocolate"*
- *"The cacao beans are"*
- *"The butter is then"*
- *"Dark chocolate is made"*
- *"Milk chocolate is made"*
- *"White chocolate is made"*

Can you see that all but the first sentence begins with the same structure? And the next three sentences are <u>exactly</u> the same! If I could even change one or two sentences, it would help make my writing sound more rhythmical. One easy way to change a sentence would be to move the transition word "then" to the beginning of the third sentence. That leaves all of my sentences pretty much the same length, though, so I think I'm going to combine the second and third sentences into a longer one: "The cacao beans are shelled, roasted, and crushed to make cocoa butter, and then the cocoa butter is heated...."

Have students turn and talk to a partner about how they might vary one of the next three sentences in the piece. Work with the students to revise the sentences in the rest of the paragraph. Continue the process of highlighting the first four words in each sentence in the next paragraph. Students should notice that the sentence beginnings are quite varied, and the sentences flow nicely. You may want to draw their attention to the technique of starting with a preposition to vary sentences—as long as they don't all start the same! Notice that three of the four sentences in the fourth paragraph start with "In" and a date. The final draft (Figure 5.7 on page 106) shows suggested revisions.

Guided Practice: Have students work in pairs to analyze the sentences in the fourth paragraph of "The Story of Chocolate." Remind them that they don't have to change every sentence in the paragraph; changing only one or two will add that little bit of variety needed to improve the cadence and flow of the writing. Suggest that they revise the first four words of at least one of the sentences in the fourth paragraph to make the writing flow more fluidly. You may want to display the paragraph or provide a copy of the draft with bookend paragraphs on page 103 for students to work with. (Again, note that Figure 5.7 offers a possible revision. As noted previously, when working with students, I make all revisions on the same draft.)

Independent Application: Have students review their own drafts, revising at least one sentence per paragraph, if necessary, to improve fluency. Students may not want to highlight their entire drafts; sometimes, simply writing out the first four words of each paragraph is a better visual for analyzing sentence beginnings.

Date

Observations

Notes for Future Instruction

Replacing Repeated Words

Another big challenge in informational writing is avoiding repetition. Certain words appear over and over again, often to the detriment of the writing. Of course, some repetition is unavoidable; certain technical words are usually essential to the topic, but developing a list of synonyms for the main topic is one way to eliminate some repetition. Another strategy is to highlight words that appear over and over in each paragraph and try to replace a few of them. It won't be possible to avoid all repetition; the goal here is to provide the necessary information while crafting it in an interesting and engaging way. In addition to varying the vocabulary, we want writers to think about making the writing sound good to the ear.

Learning Goal: Students will be able to revise their writing to vary the word choice and eliminate unnecessary repetition.

Traits: Word choice, sentence fluency

Introduction: Link the learning to students' previous experience with word choice in writing.

You've had lots of practice revising your writing to make the words more interesting and varied. Well, this is just as important with informational writing as it is with stories. In fact, sometimes it's more challenging, because we often find ourselves using certain words over and over again, especially words that describe the main topic.

In my report on chocolate, for example, I've used the word <u>chocolate</u> 28 times! Now, it isn't possible to eliminate every single repetition, especially with important technical vocabulary. But in this lesson, you are going to practice replacing some of those repeated words to make your writing sound more interesting.

Instruction: Look at the sample piece on chocolate with bookend paragraphs on page 103 or produce a clean copy for viewing and highlight the word *chocolate* every time it is used in the first paragraph. Then, demonstrate for the students how you might replace just a few of the repeated words.

What's the world's favorite flavor? If you guessed <u>chocolate</u>, you're right. In fact, the average American eats over 11 pounds of <u>chocolate</u> a year! From a tree in the rain forests of South America to the <u>chocolate</u> sauce on your ice cream, the story of <u>chocolate</u> is a fascinating one.

One technique that's helpful is to generate a list of words that you might use instead of the topic word. Have the students help you generate alternatives for *chocolate*, such as *sweet treat*, *fudge*, *candy*, *delicacy*, or *dessert*.

Think aloud as you model a process of changing some of the repeated words. It's not necessary to replace every single word, but perhaps we can revise some of them. Go back into the first paragraph and demonstrate for the students how you strike through the word you are going to replace and write the replacement word above.

I think I need to say "chocolate" in the second sentence, because that's the first time I use the word. I don't need to repeat it in the third sentence, though. I can just say "over 11 pounds of it." So, I'll cross out "chocolate" and write "it" above it. Finally, I think I'll replace "chocolate sauce" with "fudge sauce." There! I've replaced "chocolate" twice in one short paragraph to make my writing more interesting.

Continue reading the third paragraph. Because this paragraph is full of technical information, it's hard to replace words like *chocolate*, *cocoa*, and *sugar* and still retain the meaning, but invite students to turn and talk with a partner to come up with replacements for *make* and *made*.

Guided Practice: You may want to provide the students with copies of the draft with bookend paragraphs on page 103 and invite them to work in pairs on the rest of the text to see if there are other repeated words that can be replaced. (Note, for example, that the base word *drink* is used three times.) An alternative activity is to display a copy of the first draft of the piece on chocolate (see page 96) along with the final draft (see the reproducible that follows this minilesson), invite students to identify which words have been replaced, and discuss whether the replacements improve the text.

Remind students that not every use of the word *chocolate* needs to be replaced, but occasional variations keep the piece interesting. In the last paragraph, it might also be noted that I deliberately used the word *chocolate* three times in a row for effect. Word choice is about *choice*. We don't want our students arbitrarily sticking words into their writing just because the words are bigger or fancier. We do want our students to always think about what's the *best* word to convey the message.

Independent Application: Have students review their own research pieces to replace repeated words, as appropriate.

Date

Observations

Notes for Future Instruction

Final Draft: The Story of Chocolate

The Story of Chocolate

What's the world's favorite flavor? If you guessed chocolate, you're right. In fact, the average American eats over 11 pounds of it a year! But 500 years ago, most of the world had never heard of chocolate. From a tree in the rain forests of South America to the fudge sauce on your ice cream, the story of chocolate is a fascinating one.

All types of chocolate start out as beans from a tree called a cacao. The cacao beans are shelled, roasted, and crushed to make cocoa butter, and then the cocoa butter is heated to produce a thick paste called chocolate liquor. When chocolate liquor is mixed with cocoa butter and vanilla, it produces dark chocolate. Chocolate liquor, cocoa butter, sugar, and milk are combined to create milk chocolate. White chocolate contains no chocolate liquor at all—just cocoa butter with sugar and milk.

Five hundred years ago, most of the world had never tasted chocolate. In the 1500s, the Aztecs of Central America gave Christopher Columbus a spicy drink made of crushed cacao beans boiled with spices and peppers. Although he didn't much like the taste of it, Columbus brought the mixture back to Spain, where they added sugar instead of chili peppers. At that time, cacao beans were like gold, and chocolate was much too expensive for most people. But by the 1600s, chocolate houses had opened up all over Europe, and drinking chocolate became a popular pastime.

In 1847, the first chocolate bars were created by the J.S. Fry Company in England, but they tasted bitter and weren't too popular. It took another 28 years for the Swiss to figure out how to make milk chocolate. In the 1890s, American chocolate manufacturer Milton Hershey noticed children licking the coating off chocolate-covered caramels and decided to make the treat without the caramels. That was the first milk chocolate bar.

Chocolate has come a long way from its beginnings as a spicy beverage. Today there are over 30,000 kinds of chocolate candies to satisfy your sweet tooth. And if that's not enough, there is even chocolate toothpaste, chocolate pasta, and chocolate soap! No wonder it's the world's favorite flavor!

CHAPTER 6

Writing to Persuade

Is there any time of life when persuasion is more prevalent than during the school years? Every time students plead with the teacher to lighten their homework on a big game night or cajole their parents into ordering pepperoni rather than vegetarian pizza for dinner, our students are using persuasion. If there's any doubt about how pervasive persuasion is in our society, we have only to look at the number of words we have in English to describe the action of trying to bring someone to your point of view, for example, *coax, convince, entice, entreat, exhort, impel, influence, inveigle, persuade, prevail upon, reason, seduce, sell, sway, talk into, turn onto, wear down, wheedle, win over,* and *woo!*

Persuasive writing helps students learn to reason and guides them in developing logical and rational support for their ideas. It encourages writers to see the point of view of others and communicate with clarity and purpose. Finally, it provides a forum for authentic writing about topics that matter to the writer. As Barry Lane and Gretchen Bernabei (2001) assert, "We want students to have opinions, to be passionate about these opinions and to defend them with strong, well thought out and elaborated arguments" (p. 1).

Research and practice tell us that even in primary grades, children can learn to state an opinion and provide reasons for it (Wilkinson, Barnsley, Hanna, & Swan, 1980). We want intermediate students to take basic opinion writing one step further. They must learn not just to state their opinions but also to logically rationalize their opinions with a specific reader in mind. Consideration of audience is one of the key differences between simple opinion writing and effective persuasive writing. This ability to step outside of oneself and see the argument from the point of view of someone else is the big challenge for writers in grades 4–6.

It will come as no surprise to teachers that, in general, young writers are less proficient with persuasive text than with narrative text (Crowhurst, 1990). Marion Crowhurst reports that students' persuasive writing tends to suffer from poor organization and inadequate support for opinions. Part of the reason is that argumentative writing is generally considered to be more cognitively demanding than narrative writing, but let's not forget that young writers receive far less exposure to reading persuasive text than narrative text.

Crowhurst argues that it's important to include more persuasive/argumentative literacy in the elementary curriculum, because it is already so much a part of their oral language and culture.

The seven minilessons in this chapter offer a teaching sequence for taking a piece of persuasive writing from planning to publication, as described in the following section. Teaching students to write persuasive text involves the same general writing process sequence described in Chapter 5, "Researching and Writing Informational Texts," that may be adapted to any genre or text form. Through the minilessons in this chapter, I have taken the same demonstration piece, "A Battle Against Bottled Water," from prewriting to revision, along with examples of "teacher talk" that I might use in presenting the lessons to students. (The bottled water reproducible can be found on page 138.) The minilessons in this chapter could be the basis of a complete unit on persuasive writing or a menu of individual lesson choices to supplement and complement your own program (see Table 6.1 for an overview of the minilessons in this chapter).

1. ***Read and analyze samples of the genre.*** Whenever I introduce a new genre or text form, I always start by giving students an opportunity to read and analyze many text examples of the form. Children's magazines such as *Time for Kids* and *Scholastic Scope* are excellent sources for age-appropriate

TABLE 6.1. Writing to Persuade Minilessons at a Glance

Minilesson	Page	Trait(s) Addressed	Lesson Focus
Agree or Disagree?	120	Ideas	Identifying issues the writer feels strongly about
What, Why, and How Do You Know?	123	Ideas, organization	Providing reasons and explanations for an opinion
Face the Facts!	127	Ideas	Supporting an opinion with facts, statistics, and examples
Other People Might Say…	129	Ideas, organization, voice	Anticipating an argument and providing a rebuttal
AIM for a Good Opening	132	Ideas, organization, voice	Writing an effective opening paragraph
The "I, You, or We" Closing	134	Ideas, organization, voice	Writing an effective closing paragraph
Loaded Words	136	Voice, word choice	Purposefully using words that evoke emotion in a reader

persuasive and opinion writing. Engaging picture books that use persuasion include *I Wanna Iguana* by Karen Kaufman Orloff (2004), *My Brother Dan's Delicious* by Steven Layne (2003), and *Dear Mrs. LaRue: Letters From Obedience School* by Mark Teague (2002). I also keep a collection of student writing samples on hand, such as the sixth-grade piece called "I Hate Detentions!" in Figure 6.1. Invite the students to discuss what works and doesn't work in this sample text, guiding the conversation with questions such as the following:

- What do you notice about the topic and details? (strong opinion with reasons for support)
- What do you notice about how the writing is organized? (reasons listed with transition words *first*, *second*, and *third*)
- What do you notice about the opening and closing paragraphs? (strong opinion stated in the opening and restated in the closing, but lacks a grabber opening)
- What do you notice about the personality and style of the piece? What techniques did the writer use to add voice? (dialogue, exclamations, questions, emotions, passion, personal connection, and use of "I" and "you")

FIGURE 6.1. A Sixth Grader's Persuasive Writing Sample

I Hate Detentions!

I believe teachers shouldn't give detentions when kids are late! I have three good reasons why. First, sometimes teachers are late, and they just walk in like nothing happened and say, "Sorry I'm late." Then when we come in late they say, "So when I will I see you, at lunch?" or "Why are you so late?" That's not fair, and it's a double standard. Second, detentions are a huge waste of time. For example, if you are done everything and you get a detention for being late, you have to sit in an empty room for 15 minutes. Fifteen minutes doesn't sound like much. But it is if you are not doing anything. Third, my sister is really, really slow and my mom and dad make me wait for her, so she makes me late. Therefore, when I'm late because of her, it's really not my fault! For all of these reasons, I believe teachers should not give detentions because we are late.

As we read examples of the text form, we collaboratively construct a framework organized around the six traits based on the structure, organization, and language of that form. Your framework might look like this:

Ideas	Organization	Voice	Word Choice	Sentence Fluency	Conventions
• The text includes opinions that the writer feels strongly about, with reasons and evidence to support those opinions. • The evidence offered sometimes includes facts, numbers, quotes, and examples.	• Paragraphs usually open with a statement of the main point, then give support for the opinion in the body, and are followed by a conclusion that restates the argument.	• The voice is engaging and full of passion. • The text speaks to the reader.	• Words are designed to grab the reader's attention and evoke emotions. • Student uses the words *I*, *we*, and *you*.	• Sentences are interesting and varied.	• The writing conventions used are appropriate for the grade and writing level.

2. ***Identify the topic and audience for the writing.*** There are many ways to generate topics for persuasive writing. Brainstorm a list of issues of concern to intermediate students. Ask them what they would change about rules at home, at school, and in the larger world if they could. The **Agree or Disagree?** minilesson uses a graphic organizer to identify issues of concern to the students that might instigate a piece of persuasive text. In truth, the topic itself is less important than the strength with which it's developed. However, finding real causes about which to write engages and empowers young writers and may lead to more purposeful writing to authentic audiences, such as a newspaper, school board administrator, or city official.

More than any other type of writing, persuasive text is directed toward a specific audience. Before starting a piece of persuasive writing, the writer must ask himself or herself questions such as, Who am I trying to persuade? What words and ideas do I need to use in order to convince this reader to think the way I do? and What words and ideas might evoke feelings in this particular reader?

The research is mixed on intermediate students' ability to decenter their writing and focus on what their reader might be thinking (Tompkins, 2000), but Barry Kroll (1984) has found that students as young as 9 years old are able to adjust a persuasive letter for different audiences. Gail Tompkins concludes that "when students have a clear purpose and plausible reason for writing, they can adapt their writing to meet the needs of their readers" (p. 353). When writers have a meaningful topic, an authentic audience, and a clear purpose, they will write with more passion and voice, as well as be more aware of and concerned with both clarity and conventions. You may want to use the minilesson TAP Into Writing (see page 38 in Chapter 3) to teach students about identifying topic, audience, and purpose for the text.

3. *Make a plan that develops the argument with reasons and explanations.* Unlike narrative text, which is organized chronologically, and informational text, which is organized around subtopics, persuasive text is organized around reasons and explanations for a thesis or strong opinion. Writing textbooks have traditionally taught the persuasive piece as a formula: State the opinion, offer three reasons, and restate the opinion. As we see in the sample piece on detentions (see Figure 6.1, page 115), rigid structures can generate good, but rarely great, writing. In fact, Russel Durst (1984) has found that rigid formulas for writing may help students gain control of a new form, but ultimately seem to limit their continuing growth as writers. In truth, some topics require three reasons, others may have far more, and yet others may need only one compelling argument. I worry that too much emphasis on organizational structures can lead to formulaic and mundane writing.

A more flexible but still supportive structure for developing an argument is the "What-Why-How" (Peha, 1995) planning tool that was developed by Steve Peha at Teaching That Makes Sense. (A variety of uses for it may be found on their website, www.ttms.org.) **What, Why, and How Do You Know?** is based on this organizer, teaching students to state their opinions (what?), articulate reasons for their opinions (why?), and find evidence to support those reasons (how do you know?).

4. *Do some research to collect facts, examples, and statistics to support your opinion.* The "how do you know?" piece of an argument often requires writers to do some research to locate external support. Sophisticated writers know that opinions aren't effectively supported by other opinions, particularly their own. **Face the Facts!** teaches students to conduct research for facts, statistics, and examples to back up their opinions in writing.

5. *Anticipate the argument.* The most sophisticated element of persuasive writing is anticipating—and rebutting—possible opposition to one's argument. As challenging as it is to tailor one's argument to an external reader, it is even

more difficult to try to anticipate the other person's counterargument. Orloff's engaging picture book *I Wanna Iguana* is a delightful example of point and counterpoint. **Other People Might Say...** invites writers to anticipate what a reader might argue and offer additional support for their own arguments.

6. *Turn the draft into a plan.* A strong plan always makes drafting easier. The "What-Why-How" organizer (Peha, 1995) provides a strong foundation, along with evidence for support. Students can use this material to draft the body of the piece, adding the opening and closing paragraphs later. There is no consensus about how to order the arguments; some say to put the strongest point first, while others say to close with the most important point. In the end, the order of the arguments is up to the writer. Many intermediate students struggle with making the transition from a plan to a draft. As always, teacher modeling and demonstration are the best tools we have for helping students through the composition stage.

7. *Add introductory and concluding paragraphs.* When the body of a piece is complete, writers can tackle the opening and closing paragraphs. In the traditional argumentative structure, the opening paragraph states the premise or thesis, and the closing paragraph summarizes the argument. When we add an engaging lead and a satisfying ending, we have a well-crafted persuasive piece. **AIM for a Good Opening** teaches students three parts to a strong opening paragraph: Grab the reader's *attention*, provide some background *information*, and clearly state the *main point*. Usually, the concluding paragraph reiterates the key point and offers a satisfying wrap-up. **The "I, You, or We" Closing** teaches students to wrap up a piece of writing with a call to action for the reader, the writer, or both.

> ## Teaching Sequence for Persuasive Writing
>
> 1. Read and analyze samples of the genre.
> 2. Identify the topic and audience for the writing.
> 3. Make a plan that develops the argument with reasons and explanations.
> 4. Do some research to collect facts, examples, and statistics to support your opinion.
> 5. Anticipate the argument.
> 6. Turn the draft into a plan.
> 7. Add introductory and concluding paragraphs.
> 8. Revise for word choice and sentence fluency.
> 9. Polish and publish.

8. *Revise for word choice and sentence fluency.* After completing the draft, students will need to revisit, review, and revise their piece of writing for clarity and voice. This is the time to consider whether the language and tone of the writing speaks effectively to a reader. Well-chosen vocabulary can contribute significantly to persuading someone else to our point of view. **Loaded Words** teaches students to purposefully use words that generate emotional responses above and beyond the words' intended meanings (Engel, 2000). Loaded words elicit a response—positive or negative—from a reader. For example, the noun *plant* generally carries no emotional baggage, whereas *rose* usually inspires a positive reaction, and *weed* carries a negative connotation. As your students will realize, advertising is full of loaded words, such as *new, improved,* and

better. Judicious use of loaded words in persuasive writing can help influence a reader to come around to our way of thinking.

9. ***Polish and publish.*** Once the writing says what the writer wants it to say, the way the writer wants to say it, the piece may be edited and polished for publication. The publication of persuasive writing can take many forms, from a letter to an editorial. As always, an authentic audience is the best incentive for powerful writing.

Persuasive writing can help students make a difference in their world. At age 9, Severn Cullis-Suzuki and some friends started the Environmental Children's Organization, and at age 12, she gave a powerful speech to the United Nations Earth Summit in Rio de Janeiro. Craig Kielburger was only 12 years old when he read an article about child labor and gathered a group of kids to found Free the Children. Severn and Craig not only took on a cause but also persuaded others to join them. All over the world, students as young as fourth, fifth, and sixth grades are making a difference in the world. Your students could do the same.

NOTES

Date

_____

Observations

_____
_____
_____
_____
_____
_____
_____
_____
_____

Notes for Future Instruction

_____
_____
_____
_____
_____
_____
_____
_____
_____
_____
_____

Agree or Disagree?

The first step in any type of writing is choosing a topic. This lesson uses an Agree or Disagree? chart to help students find issues that matter most to them. You may wish to use the reproducible chart at the end of this minilesson or create a chart with your students that includes issues of specific relevance to them.

Learning Goal: Students will be able to choose topics for persuasive writing by identifying issues that they feel most strongly about.

Trait: Ideas

Introduction: Link to students' prior knowledge of the structures of persuasive writing. Remind them that good persuasive writing starts with a strong opinion.

An opinion is an idea that a person believes in or doesn't believe in. Everyone has different opinions. You might believe that pepperoni is the best type of pizza in the world, but another person might hate pepperoni pizza. Neither of you is right or wrong; you just have different opinions. That's the difference between a fact and an opinion. A fact is true: Maple trees lose their leaves in the fall. An opinion is what someone believes: Maple leaves are the prettiest kind of leaf. In this lesson, you'll have a chance to think about some opinions and whether you agree or disagree with them.

Instruction: Tell students that today they will be looking at a list of opinions and will have to indicate whether they strongly agree, mildly agree, strongly disagree, mildly disagree, or are indifferent to each one. Provide each student with a copy of the reproducible Agree or Disagree? chart on page 122 (or one of your own). Read the first statement aloud:

"Girls and boys should be in separate classes in school."

Talk about the difference between "strongly agree" and "mildly agree," or "strongly disagree" and "mildly disagree." Invite students to indicate their selections on their own charts.

If you are concerned about students being able to read or understand all the words, feel free to read them aloud as the students complete their charts. Have students check or color in the box in each row that represents their feelings about the issue.

After the students have completed their individual charts, have them look down the "strongly agree" column and highlight every opinion that they have checked or colored in that column. Then, with a different color, have them highlight all the opinions that they checked in the "strongly disagree" column.

The opinions from your "strongly agree" or "strongly disagree" columns are the ones that will make the best topics for your writing. Because they're the ones you care most about, you will be able to put more feeling and voice into your writing.

Guided Practice: Invite students to turn and talk to a partner about their strongest opinions. Suggest that they try to give their partners reasons for their opinions. This will help them decide which topics they will be able to support most effectively in their writing. You may want to use the **Tell It Twice** strategy (see page 43) to have students talk to two different partners about their opinions.

Independent Application: Have students store their Agree or Disagree? charts in their writing folders to use as potential writing topics.

Date

Observations

Notes for Future Instruction

Agree or Disagree?

Opinions	Strongly Agree	Mildly Agree	Don't Agree or Disagree	Mildly Disagree	Strongly Disagree
1. Girls and boys should be in separate classes in school.					
2. Online schools would be just as good for learning as traditional schools.					
3. Computers don't really help kids learn.					
4. Video games make kids more violent.					
5. Kids should be allowed to have cell phones at school.					
6. Children under 9 should not be allowed to use the Internet.					
7. Scientists should be able to use animals for testing products.					
8. You should have to get a license to chop down a tree.					
9. Seat belts aren't necessary for people riding in the back seat of a car.					
10. It should be illegal to wear fur coats.					
11. It's possible to be too thin.					
12. There is life on other planets.					
13. There should be no zoos.					
14. Smoking should be against the law.					

What, Why, and How Do You Know?

When students plan a piece of persuasive writing, we want them to think about reasons for their opinion or belief and about support for those reasons. This lesson asks writers to plan "what?" (the opinion or issue), "why?" (reasons for the opinion), and "how do you know?" (evidence to support the reasons).

Your intermediate students are sure to take great delight in a read-aloud of David Wisniewski's (1998) *The Secret Knowledge of Grown-Ups*, which is a book about some common rules that adults set for kids. According to the author, there is always an "official" reason for each of the rules, but there's also a "secret" reason that only grown-ups know. Not only is this an engaging picture book, but also it is a good structure for introducing opinions, reasons, and evidence.

This lesson is actually more than a one-day minilesson. Ideally, the What, Why, and How Do You Know? charting of *The Secret Knowledge of Grown-Ups* would be done in the reading block, and the planning for the students' own writing would be done in the writing block.

Learning Goal: Students will be able to use a prewriting organizer to plan their opinions, support, and evidence.

Traits: Ideas, organization

Introduction: Review previous discussions of the nature of opinions and their importance in persuasive writing. Tell students that a strong opinion is just the starting point for good persuasive writing. They also need reasons for their opinions and evidence to support those reasons. In this lesson, students will be learning about the "what, why, and how do you know?" of writing.

Instruction: Display the reproducible What, Why, and How Do You Know? chart provided at the end of this minilesson to reinforce the three key elements of persuasion. Choose a section of the book *The Secret Knowledge of Grown-Ups* (it isn't necessary to read the entire book for this lesson), then choose one of the "rules" to read aloud, and together complete the chart. Here is an example:

What?	Why?	How Do You Know?
Don't pick your nose.	It might cause your brain to deflate.	Scientists have found an air pipeline from your nose to a pumping station that keeps your brain inflated. If you pick your nose, you could dent or poke a hole in this pipe, causing the air to leak out of your brain.

Note that often there will be more than one "why" or more than one "how," but there is no formula for the number. It really depends on the key idea of the writing.

Work collaboratively to summarize a couple of the book's "rules" in the chart. You may want to provide groups of two or three students with one of the rules and have them summarize the what, why, and how for that rule.

Guided Practice: Have the students use the same structure to practice completing a What, Why, and How Do You Know? chart for a class book called "The Secret Knowledge of Teachers."

We've read about David Wiesniewski's ideas about the secret reasons parents have for the rules for kids. Do you suppose there is also a secret knowledge of teachers? What do you think might be the secret reasons behind some of the rules we have in school?

With the students, make a list of school rules. Have students work in pairs or small groups to choose a rule and complete a What, Why, and How Do You Know? chart about the "secret" reasons behind it (see the example in Figure 6.2). Note that because the purpose of this exercise is to give students practice in articulating reasons and support for an idea, the completion of the What, Why, and How Do You Know? chart is the intended end result.

FIGURE 6.2. Sample Text for "The Secret Knowledge of Teachers"

School Rule: Students should not wear hats in school.
"Official" Reason: It's bad manners
Secret Knowledge of Teachers:

What?	Why?	How Do You Know?
Students should not wear hats in school	It ruins your appearrance.	Fact: Wearing a hat causes "hat head" in 100% of cases.
	It stifles your thinking.	Dr. I.M. Bald from Brainy University has found that people who wear hats have only half as many good ideas as people who don't wear hats.

Note. Adapted from *The Secret Knowledge of Grown-Ups*, by D. Wisniewski, 1998, New York: Lothrop, Lee & Shepard.

Independent Application: Have students select one of their strong opinions from their Agree or Disagree? chart and complete a What, Why, and How Do You Know? planner (see the example in Figure 6.3). It's a good idea to have students complete at least three charts, so they solidify their understanding of articulating reasons and explanations for their opinions. This will also enable them to choose the topic that best lends itself to strong, cogent arguments.

FIGURE 6.3. Sample What, Why, and How Do You Know? Chart on Bottled Water

What?	Why?	How Do You Know?
People should stop using bottled water.	It's hard on the environment.	• I don't like the mess when people just litter. • Fewer than 20% of plastic bottles in the United States are recycled. The rest fill up landfills, taking hundreds of years to decompose.
	It costs too much.	• Tap water costs next to nothing, but a bottle of water costs anywhere from 50¢ to $2 or more. • People have better things to do with their money.

Date

Observations

Notes for Future Instruction

What, Why, and How Do You Know?

What? (opinion or main point)	Why? (reasons for the opinion)	How do you know? (explanations, evidence, statistics, facts)

Face the Facts!

Finding evidence to support an opinion can be a big challenge for intermediate writers. All too often, they find themselves supporting an opinion with another opinion, such as "I don't think we should have homework, because I don't like doing schoolwork at night." Unfortunately, this kind of reasoning doesn't go far in persuasive writing. This minilesson teaches students to use facts, examples, and statistics to support their reasoning.

Conducting research for evidence to back up their arguments is excellent practice for our students. You'll have to decide the format you want your students to use when citing sources. Although footnoting and citations are generally not taught until upper grades, it is a good model for students to acknowledge at least authors, titles, copyright dates, and URL addresses.

Learning Goal: Students will be able to research facts, examples, and statistics to support their opinions and reasons.

Trait: Ideas

Introduction: Invite students to look at the sample What, Why, and How Do You Know? chart (Figure 6.3, page 125). Have them turn and talk about which of these pieces of evidence is stronger:

- "I don't like the mess when people just litter."
- "Fewer than 20% of plastic bottles in the United States are recycled. The rest fill up landfills, taking hundreds of years to decompose."

Talk about the difference between the two statements. The first is just another opinion, whereas the second is a fact. In this minilesson, students will practice identifying and researching facts, numbers, and examples to support their arguments.

Instruction: Continue the discussion with the second "why?" in the chart. Elicit from students that the strongest evidence ("how do you know?") comes from facts, numbers, or specific examples.

To clarify the meaning of *specific*, use examples such as these:

- Americans buy a lot of bottled water.
- Americans buy about 30 billion bottles of bottled water every year.

The second example is more powerful, because it gives a specific detail with a statistic. Basically, statistics are numbers (how many?, how much?, how often?).

Date

Observations

Notes for Future Instruction

When we give specific details, we add power to our arguments. It's also a good idea to tell where the statistic came from, so the reader doesn't think the writer just made it up, for example, "According to a New York state government website, Americans purchased almost 31 billion bottles of water in 2006 alone."

Share the sample paragraphs in Figure 6.4 with your students. Invite them to look for a general statement in paragraph 1 that would be stronger with some statistics to back it up. Point out words and phrases like *lots* and *small number*. Discuss with students why specific numbers would be more effective.

Review the revised paragraph (paragraph 2 in Figure 6.4) with the students. Have them identify specific statistics in this paragraph.

Guided Practice: Have students work in partners to highlight specific facts and statistics in paragraph 3 of Figure 6.4.

Independent Application: Have students research facts and statistics to insert into their What, Why, and How Do You Know? planners.

FIGURE 6.4. Sample Paragraphs for Fact Finding

Paragraph 1

I think people should stop drinking bottled water, because it is bad for the environment. Lots of empty water bottles are ending up in landfills and garbage dumps—and even in the ocean. Only a small number are being recycled. This doesn't even include the environmental impact of producing, filling, and packaging the bottles for sale.

Paragraph 2

Bottled water is damaging to the environment. Fewer than 20% of plastic bottles in the United States are recycled. The rest fill up landfills, taking hundreds of years to decompose. Scientists report that there is an island of discarded plastic in the Pacific Ocean that is more than twice the size of Texas. Even the production of plastic bottles for sale uses up 50 million barrels of oil each year and sends up to three tons of carbon dioxide into our atmosphere.

Paragraph 3

Another good reason to stop using bottled water is that it is so expensive. Tap water costs next to nothing, but a bottle of water costs anywhere from 50¢ to $2 or more. In fact, a gallon of bottled water costs more than a gallon of gasoline! Most of that money is not to pay for the water itself; it's for packaging, advertising, and selling. Americans spend over $15 billion a year on bottled water—and that's over and above what they've already paid in taxes for their own tap water. Most families have better things to do with their money.

Other People Might Say...

Anticipating—and countering—an opposing argument takes persuasive writing to a higher level. This minilesson provides students with practice in thinking about what other people might argue—and practice in providing a rebuttal to those arguments. Not all of our intermediate writers will be able to step outside of themselves enough to think from the reader's perspective. Teachers should assess their students' readiness before expecting them to anticipate the argument.

Learning Goal: Students will be able to develop and counter a possible argument against their opinions.

Traits: Ideas, organization, voice

Introduction: Revisit the importance of speaking to an audience in persuasive writing.

One of the hardest things about persuasive writing is guessing what our reader is thinking! We want to give our readers information that supports our opinion, but we also need to predict what reasons they might have for disagreeing with us. That way, we can offer arguments against their arguments <u>before</u> they even argue with us! Anticipating the reader's argument—and arguing against it—puts you a step ahead of the reader in persuading him or her to your point of view.

In this lesson, you're going to learn to think about what other people might say against your opinion, so you can present reasons against their thinking.

Instruction: Display the paragraphs in Figure 6.5 and talk your students through the process of anticipating arguments.

I think I've got some pretty good arguments about why people should stop using bottled water. I have a bunch of statistics about how bottled water is harming the environment. I've got some facts about the cost of bottled water compared to tap water. Now, I need to try to predict what argument a reader might give. Turn and talk with a partner about what arguments someone might have in favor of bottled water.

Some arguments in favor of bottled water might include the following:

- *It tastes better.*
- *It's better for you.*
- *You can always have it on hand, even when there's no water fountain.*

I could argue against any of these points, but I'm going to choose the statement that bottled water is better for you than tap water. Here are some of the facts I've learned from my reading:

- *Lots of bottled water is just tap water in bottles.*
- *Many cities add fluoride to their tap water, which is good for our teeth.*
- *Most cities monitor the quality of their public water.*

Next, I'm going to add another paragraph to my writing.

Share with students the added paragraph anticipating arguments (see Figure 6.6).

FIGURE 6.5. Sample Paragraphs to Begin Anticipating Arguments

I think people should stop using bottled water, because it is damaging to the environment. Less than 20% of plastic bottles in the United States are recycled. The rest fill up landfills, taking hundreds of years to decompose. Scientists report that there is an island of discarded plastic in the Pacific Ocean that is more than twice the size of Texas. Even the production of plastic bottles for sale uses up 50 million barrels of oil each year and sends up to three tons of carbon dioxide into our atmosphere.

Another good reason to stop using bottled water is that it is so expensive. Tap water costs next to nothing, but a bottle of water can cost anywhere from 50¢ to $2 or more. In fact, a gallon of bottled water costs more than a gallon of gasoline! Most of that money is not to pay for the water itself. It's for packaging, advertising, and selling. Americans spend over $15 billion a year on bottled water—and that's over and above what they've already paid in taxes for their own tap water. Most families have better things to do with their money.

FIGURE 6.6. Paragraph Added to Rebut Arguments

Some people argue that bottled water is healthier for you than tap water. In truth, much of the water that we buy in bottles is actually just tap water! Sometimes it has been purified, but not always. In some ways, tap water is even better for you. For example, many cities add fluoride to their tap water, which prevents cavities and tooth decay. In most places, tap water is more carefully monitored for bacteria than bottled water is. But, does it taste better? One television program surveyed people in New York to see which water they preferred, and most of them chose the tap water!

Guided Practice: Revisit the student sample piece "I Hate Detentions!" (Figure 6.1, page 115). Have students work in small groups to add an "other people might say" argument.

Independent Application: Have students add an "other people might say" argument and counterargument to their planner or draft, depending on the stage of their writing.

NOTES

Date

Observations

Notes for Future Instruction

AIM for a Good Opening

The opening paragraph in a piece of persuasive writing serves two purposes: to grab the reader's attention and to introduce the premise or opinion. The acronym *AIM* suggests three essential parts of the introductory paragraph: attention grabber, important background information, and the major point.

Learning Goal: Students will be able to craft an effective opening paragraph with an attention getter, background information, and the main point.

Traits: Ideas, organization, voice

Introduction: Show students these two different openings for a piece of persuasive writing about year-round schooling. Have them turn and talk about which opening is more interesting and why.

- I think school should run all year long.
- Rrring! Rrring! All over the country, the bells of September are ringing—and you know what that means. Kids are returning to school after the long summer break.

The first example just states the writer's opinion. It's the main point of the piece, but it certainly isn't a grabber. In fact, instead of grabbing a reader's attention, some people might actually <u>stop</u> reading at this point! The second example grabs our attention, but doesn't tell us what the piece is about. A good opening paragraph needs to do both—grab the reader's attention <u>and</u> state the main point. In this lesson, you're going to learn a technique for writing good opening paragraphs.

Instruction: We have already looked at two important parts of the introductory paragraph: the attention grabber and the opinion or main point. Now we need some background information to link the two pieces together. Display the paragraph in Figure 6.7 for students and talk them through the ways this paragraph demonstrates how to craft a good beginning.

This paragraph shows us how we can "AIM" for a great beginning. <u>A</u> stands for <u>attention grabber</u>. What's the attention grabber here? The <u>M</u> in AIM stands for the <u>main point</u> or opinion of the piece. Who can identify the main point? The middle letter in AIM is <u>I</u>, and that stands for <u>information</u>. We need some background information as a bridge between the attention grabber and the main point. That's why I've added a fact about kids losing learning over the long summer break. Turn and talk to a partner about what AIM stands for.

FIGURE 6.7. Sample Good Opening Paragraph

Rrring! Rrring! All over the country, the bells of September are ringing—and you know what that means. Kids all over the country are returning to school after the long summer break. For the last eight weeks or more, these kids have been playing video and computer games, and running and swimming and biking outdoors—pretty much doing everything but reading. Test scores show that many kids are actually losing a lot of learning over the long summer break. That's why I think school should run all year long.

Model and think aloud as you construct an opening paragraph for a persuasive piece, or use the reproducible sample piece on bottled water on page 138 with the lead and conclusion deleted. (You may want to revisit the minilesson **Add Some Bling!** on page 104 in Chapter 5 for ideas for grabber openings.)

Let's look at my piece on bottled water. I've got the main point ("I think people should stop using bottled water"), but I need an attention grabber. Here's an <u>amazing</u> fact: According to a website called Earth911.com, Americans buy almost 30 <u>billion</u> plastic water bottles every year (that's five for every person in the entire world), and 8 out of every 10 will end up in landfills or the ocean! Now, how can I turn that into a grabber beginning?

- <u>Attention grabber:</u> Try to picture 30 <u>billion</u> plastic bottles.
- <u>Information:</u> That's how many bottles of water Americans buy <u>every year</u>—and three quarters of those bottles will end up in landfills or the ocean!
- <u>Main point:</u> This is just one reason why I think people should stop using plastic water bottles.

Guided Practice: Display the following three statements for students. Have them work in pairs or small groups to choose one and construct an AIM beginning.

- Wild animals do not make good pets.
- Kids should be able to go to bed whenever they want.
- Everyone should wear a helmet when riding a bike.

Independent Application: Have students create AIM paragraphs for their own writing pieces.

The "I, You, or We" Closing

I like to say that a good ending is like the bow on a present: It just wraps the piece up neatly. An effective conclusion for persuasive writing generally summarizes the argument and often ends with a call to action—an "I, you, or we" statement.

Learning Goal: Students will be able to craft an effective closing paragraph for a piece of persuasive writing.

Traits: Ideas, organization, voice

Introduction: Remind students that they have already written the beginning and middle of a piece, but it isn't complete without an effective ending. Use the completed bottled water piece on page 138 as an example, with the ending paragraph removed. Review with the students the structures that are already in place in this piece.

So far, we've got an opening that grabs the reader's attention, provides some background information, and identifies the main point. We've added some solid arguments, backed by facts and statistics. We've even noted an argument that other people might say and argued against it. Now, the only thing missing is a satisfying ending that wraps the piece up neatly and leaves the reader understanding and—you hope—believing in your point of view. In this lesson, you will learn about ending a piece of persuasive writing.

Instruction: Use the sample bottled water text on page 138 as a model or create one of your own. Display paragraph 5, the conclusion, for the students. Point out that the first sentence summarizes the arguments that have been made in the body of the piece. It reviews the key point for the reader. The next two sentences suggest an action that the reader can take. A call to action suggests something that the writer (I), the reader (you), or both (we) can do. A good way to end a piece of persuasive writing is by making an "I, you, or we" statement.

> Bottled water is damaging to the environment, to our bodies, and to our wallets. The next time you want to take some water to the beach, on a run, or for a ride in the car, grab a reusable sports bottle, dip it under the kitchen faucet, and off you go. You'll be doing some good for your body and for the earth.

Guided Practice: Revisit the piece "I Hate Detentions!" (Figure 6.1, page 115). Students will note that it already ends with a summary statement,

FIGURE 6.8. Sentence Starters for Reviewing the Main Point in the Summary

- For all of these reasons…
- As you can see,…
- I'm sure you'll agree that…
- It's clear that…
- Without question,…
- All in all,…
- In conclusion,…

which the writer began with "For all of these reasons." Some sample starters for a summary statement are found in Figure 6.8. Have the students work in pairs or small groups to come up with a call to action—an "I, you, or we" statement.

Independent Application: Have students craft a closing paragraph for their own piece of writing.

Date

Observations

Notes for Future Instruction

Loaded Words

Loaded words are words that evoke emotion in a reader. They may arouse positive feelings, such as *new, better,* or *healthy,* or negative emotions, such as *fail* or *pollution.* Whether a word is loaded or not often depends on the context and the reader. For example, the word *pig* may have a negative connotation for some, a positive one for others, and no emotional response at all from yet others. That's why it's always important for a writer to know his or her audience, so he or she can use words that have a particular connection for that reader. This minilesson provides students with practice in identifying and using loaded words.

This minilesson could be presented at any point during the unit. You may want to make students aware of the concept before they begin to draft. I've chosen to put this lesson at the end of the unit, as part of the revision process.

Learning Goal: Students will be able to identify and purposefully use vocabulary that evokes emotion in the reader.

Traits: Voice, word choice

Introduction: Revisit the importance of audience in persuasive writing.

When we write to persuade someone about an issue, it's important to include ideas and reasons to go along with our thinking, but we also need to think about the words we use. Certain words can help make readers feel positive or negative about an idea. For example, using words like <u>healthy</u> or <u>safe</u> causes a positive reaction from most people. Words like <u>germs</u> or <u>caution</u> might cause a negative reaction. We call these <u>loaded words</u>, because they can generate emotions or feelings. Today, you're going to learn about using loaded words to make your writing more persuasive.

Instruction: With your students, examine a piece of advertising or a brochure from a tourist attraction. Invite the students to identify words that make a reader want to buy that product or visit that place. The students are likely to come up with words like *fun, family, sparkling, free,* and *exciting.*

The words and arguments we use may vary from one piece of writing to another, depending on who the reader is. For example, I'm going to write a brochure to persuade someone to visit an amusement park. If I use words like <u>exciting</u>, <u>wild</u>, <u>fastest</u>, and <u>highest</u>, would I be more likely to be speaking to a senior citizen or a teenager?

FIGURE 6.9. Sample List of Loaded Words

better	educational	new	safe
dangerous	environment	nuisance	science
delicious	exciting	raw	wild
delight	horrify		

Display the list of loaded words in Figure 6.9. Have students turn and talk with a partner about which words are positive, which ones are negative, and which are neutral. (Then revisit paragraphs 2–4 in the sample text on bottled water on page 138.)

I decided at the start that the audience for my piece on bottled water was going to be families—parents and kids. I want to make sure I've used some loaded words that give them strong feelings toward my topic. Some examples of loaded words (and phrases) might be <u>healthy</u>, <u>good for you</u>, and <u>safe</u>. Loaded words that create negative feelings might be <u>germs</u>, <u>dangerous</u>, <u>irresponsible</u>, and <u>pollution</u>. Both kinds of words work to create emotion in my reader, make them feel something about the topic, and hopefully win them to my way of thinking.

Guided Practice: Provide students with a copy of the bottled water text on page 138. Have them work with a partner to highlight some of the loaded words that they notice in the piece about bottled water that is directed to an audience of families with children. Have them discuss with their partners whether these words have positive or negative connotations.

The loaded words and phrases might include *damaging, environment, hundreds of years to decompose, discarded plastic, atmosphere, expensive, taxes, better things to do, healthier, purified, bacteria,* and *good for your body*. There are no right or wrong answers; if a word or phrase evokes emotion, it's a loaded word.

Independent Application: Have students highlight any words they consider to be loaded words in their own writing and revise the piece where appropriate to insert words intended to evoke emotion in the reader.

Final Draft: A Battle Against Bottled Water

A Battle Against Bottled Water

Try to picture 30 *billion* plastic bottles. That's five times as many bottles as there are people in the entire world. That's how many bottles of water Americans buy *every year*, and three quarters of those bottles will end up in landfills or the ocean! This is just one of the reasons why I think it's time to stop using plastic water bottles.

Bottled water is damaging to the environment. Less than 20% of plastic bottles in the United States are recycled. The rest fill up landfills, taking hundreds of years to decompose. Scientists report that there is an island of discarded plastic in the Pacific Ocean that is more than twice the size of Texas. Even the production of plastic bottles for sale uses up 50 million barrels of oil each year and sends up to three tons of carbon dioxide into our atmosphere.

Another good reason to stop using bottled water is that it is so expensive. Tap water costs next to nothing, but a bottle of water can cost anywhere from 50¢ to $2 or more. In fact, a gallon of bottled water costs more than a gallon of gasoline! Most of that money is not to pay for the water itself; it's for packaging, advertising, and selling. Americans spend over $15 billion a year on bottled water—and that's over and above what they've already paid in taxes for their own tap water. Most families have better things to do with their money.

Some people argue that bottled water is healthier and tastes better than tap water. In truth, much of the water that we buy in bottles is actually just tap water! Sometimes it has been purified, but not always. In some ways, tap water is even better for you. For example, many cities add fluoride to tap water to prevent cavities and tooth decay. In most places, tap water is more carefully monitored for bacteria than bottled water is. But, does it taste better? Showtime Television gave people in New York a hidden taste test of bottled versus tap water, and 75% of them actually preferred the taste of the tap water!

Bottled water is damaging to the environment, to our bodies, and to our wallets. The next time you want to take a drink to the beach, on a run, or for a ride in the car, grab a reusable sports bottle, dip it under the kitchen faucet, and off you go. You'll be doing some good for your body and for the earth.

Marvelous Minilessons for Teaching Intermediate Writing, Grades 4–6 by Lori Jamison Rog. © 2011 International Reading Association. May be copied for classroom use.

CHAPTER 7

The Writer's Craft: Writing With Rhythm and Flair

The previous chapters of this book deal mainly with helping students develop the content of writing: choosing a topic, making a plan, and elaborating on ideas. This chapter examines the craft of writing—not so much *what* the writer says but *how* the writer says it.

Look at the poem in Figure 7.1, which was written by a sixth grader. She handpicked every word: the vivid verbs, the rhythmical phrases, the

---

FIGURE 7.1. A Sixth Grader's Poem

<u>Maui Dreams</u>
By Jennifer

I watch the morning sun
set the sky on fire
over the mountain.
I bask on the beach,
soaking up the sun.
I splash in the salty surf.
I scan the horizon
for the silhouettes
of breaching whales
and diving dolphins.

Black sand tickles my toes
as I stroll along the beach.
Windsurfers' neon sails
skim across the shimmering sea.
I watch the sun
drop below the horizon
leaving the island in darkness.
The alarm clock rings.
It's back to reality.
Fifty below in Saskatchewan.

---

varied sentences, and the surprise ending. Here is a young writer who knows something about craft.

Craft has been variously defined as style, polish, and eloquence. Back in 1910, in *The Craftsmanship of Writing* (still available today), Frederic Taber Cooper (1910/1920) wrote, "Style...means the ability to choose the words that will give us just the right meaning, just the right harmony, just the right cadence" (pp. 228–229). This chapter will focus on the way writers choose and use words to give their writing fluency and flair. We want students to think about not just the individual words they use but also how they put those words together in phrases, sentences, and even paragraphs. We want them to vary sentences, play with vocabulary, and find the "just right" rather than the "good enough" combination of words.

The seven minilessons in this chapter progress from individual words to phrases to sentences to paragraphs (see Table 7.1 for an overview of the minilessons in this chapter). The minilessons take students into both professional and student writing to hunt for words and analyze literary techniques. From literary models to guided practice with modified cloze and revision activities, we want students to learn to recognize and apply the elements of craft to their own writing.

When it comes to choosing words, most students tend to think that bigger is better. In reality, however, the *best* word isn't necessarily the fanciest word.

TABLE 7.1. The Writer's Craft: Writing With Rhythm and Flair Minilessons at a Glance

Minilesson	Page	Trait(s) Addressed	Lesson Focus
Vivid Verbs Bring Writing to Life	146	Word choice	Replacing mundane verbs and verb/adverb phrases with vivid verbs
The Magic of Three	149	Word choice, sentence fluency	Putting words, phrases, and ideas in groups of three for fluency and rhythm
Say It With a Simile	152	Ideas, word choice	Using unusual comparisons, especially similes
Pop in a Popper	154	Ideas, word choice	Inserting a descriptive phrase to modify a noun
Three-Sentence Stories	157	Ideas, sentence fluency	Combining sentence types: declarative, interrogative, and imperative
Flip the Sentence	161	Word choice, sentence fluency, conventions	Revising the order of phrases in a sentence
The Five Ps of Paragraphing	165	Organization, conventions	Paragraphing narrative text

As Mark Twain famously said, "The difference between the *almost*-right word & the *right* word is really a large matter—it's the difference between the lightning-bug & the lightning." We want young writers to use resources for word choice without developing "thesaurusitis," that dreaded syndrome of synonymous words that don't necessarily fit the context of the writing, as in "He aspired to dry his hair before ascending to the dinner table" (Spandel, 2001, p. 39). Let's face it, pretentious verbiage is often repellant to the typical peruser of print; in other words, too many fancy words can send a reader running for the hills!

Powerful verbs and precise nouns are the foundations of word choice. The minilesson **Vivid Verbs Bring Writing to Life** guides students through retiring tired verbs, in other words, replacing the mundane with the fresh, the lethargic with the energetic, the bland with the brilliant. It has been suggested that if a writer needs to use an adverb, he or she probably hasn't used a strong enough verb. In fact, author Stephen King (2000) has gone so far as to say, "The road to hell is paved with adverbs" (p. 118). Why say "walked slowly" when you can use "trudged," "meandered," or "strolled"? I'm not suggesting that all modifiers should be eradicated. Adjectives and adverbs can add color and clarity to nouns and verbs, but they can also clutter up writing if used indiscriminately. Teacher Trent Lorcher (2010) states in his blog, "When revising, treat adverbs and adjectives as you would an uninvited guest at a party. You don't have to kick all of them out, but some are just up to no good and need to go" (para. 14).

Gift of a Word

A technique that works wonders for getting students to transfer interesting words from their reading to their writing is what I call "gift of a word." I provide students with sticky notes on which to write powerful words from their reading. They must leave these notes in their writing folders until they have used the word in their writing. Only when they have used a word can they pass it along as a "gift" to someone else. The new student then must keep the sticky note in his or her writing folder until he or she uses it, then he or she can pass it along to yet another person.

There's something about our English language that lends itself to threes. Putting words and ideas in a group of three can add rhythm and cadence to the sound of the language and add inspiration and passion to the message. Benjamin Franklin once wrote, "Tell me and I forget. Teach me and I remember. Involve me and I learn." Not only was this a worthy sentiment, but also it was a powerful rhetorical technique. A series of three parallel words, phrases, or clauses is known as a *tricolon* in literary parlance. I like to call it the "magic of three." U.S. President Barack Obama's (2009) inaugural speech was peppered with tricolons; who could fail to be inspired by statements like, "I stand here today humbled by the task before us, grateful for the trust you've bestowed, mindful of the sacrifices borne by our ancestors" (para. 1)? Tricolons are easy to read, easy to say, and easy to remember. See what I mean? With **The Magic of Three**, students will learn how to apply this useful writing technique to make their writing more engaging, fluent, and rhythmical.

According to children's author Norton Juster (1989), what's "as varied as snowflakes, as handy as tacks, as thrilling as danger, unlikely as yaks" (n.p.)? If you said a simile, you're right! Grammatically speaking, a simile draws a comparison between two ideas using the word *like* or *as*. When writers use similes in writing, they help readers see something in a new light by associating it with something else. Unfortunately, some similes have become overused to the point of becoming clichés: busy as a bee, quiet as a mouse, sings like a bird. The goal of **Say It With a Simile** is to help students understand and recognize this literary device and create fresh and original similes to enhance their own writing. Although the same lesson structure could also be used to introduce metaphors or personification, I find that similes are easiest for intermediate students to grasp, so I start with similes (and that would be alliteration!).

Pop in a Popper introduces the appositive: a group of words inserted after a noun to modify that noun. There, I just did it. I added "a group of words inserted after a noun" to define the word *popper*. In simplest terms, we pop this group of words into a sentence to tell more about a noun. Unlike an adjective, which goes before a noun in English, a popper is popped in after the noun. Technically speaking, an appositive restates the noun to which it refers and does not contain a verb. We're going to be a little more liberal with our definition to allow a verb, adjective, or prepositional phrase that "sharpens the image, amplifying it with new information and clarifying the meaning for the reader" (Anderson, 2007, pp. 114–115). Like an appositive, a popper is embedded in a sentence, separated from the basic subject and predicate by commas, as in "Jennifer, my best friend, lives down the street," or "It was just an ordinary street, framed by picket fences and manicured lawns, but it was my home." (Sometimes poppers might be separated from the rest of the sentence by dashes—an additional punctuation complication—but we'll focus on commas for now.) It's also important to remember that the sentence itself is intact if you pop out the popper.

Of course, good writing is not just about words. Writers must group those words into special structures called sentences. Why are so many students confused about sentences? Maybe it's because someone has told them that a sentence is a complete thought. That has to be one of the most misleading things we teachers tell students! I would argue that we have lots of complete thoughts that aren't complete sentences (for example, "Oh, no!" "Not again!" "Guilty."). Let's face it, there are plenty of grammatically correct sentences that, taken out of context, are pretty incomplete to a reader or listener; such as, "The llama smeared lipstick on her lips and applied mascara on her toenails." There's nothing wrong with this sentence grammatically, but I think we're missing a few things here in terms of a complete thought. It seems to me that a complete thought is more about context and a sentence is more about grammatical structure. A sentence is a special group of words that must have a subject (who or what) and a predicate (is or does). (Technically, this group of words is called a clause, and a sentence consists of one or more clauses.) Once students have that foundational understanding, they can create, build, embellish, and flip sentences to their hearts' content.

Varying sentence structure and length can add fluency and rhythm to a piece of writing, as well as interest and shape to the piece of writing as a whole. There are four main ways that writers can vary sentences:

1. *Vary sentence types.* Sentence variety is pretty simple when you realize that there are only four main types of sentences: declarative (statement), interrogative (question), exclamatory, and imperative (command). Although the majority of sentences in a text will be declarative, inserting a question or exclamation can add voice and interest to the piece. The **Three-Sentence Stories** minilesson provides practice in using different sentence types by having students tell a story using only three different sentences.

2. *Vary sentence structure.* Too much student writing suffers from "sluggish sentence syndrome"—sentence after sentence following the same subject–predicate, subject–predicate, subject–predicate pattern. **Flip the Sentence** combines instruction in writer's craft, grammar, and punctuation as students learn to identify chunks of words, such as prepositional phrases and subordinate clauses, and practice changing the order of the "chunk" and the "kernel" of the sentence to add rhythm, variety, and interest.

3. *Vary sentence beginnings.* Even changing the first few words can make a difference to sentence fluency. Chapter 5 contains a minilesson called **The First Four Words: Making Your Sentences Flow**, in which students revise their informational writing by analyzing the first four words of each sentence (see page 107). Another technique for varying sentence beginnings is to start with a preposition. Teach students that a preposition is a word that relates a pronoun or noun to another word in the sentence; for example, *under* a tree or *in* the morning. Lists of prepositions may be found with a simple Internet search and can provide students with a range of tools for sentence variety.

4. *Vary sentence lengths.* Generally speaking, we tend to use long, flowing sentences for description and short, quick sentences for action. Writers can use sentence length to guide the reader slowly or whirl the reader through the text. Too many sentences of the same length and structure can create monotony. Reading a lengthy text with too many periods is a lot like driving in stop-and-start traffic. But if all sentences are too long, the writing can become unwieldy, and we may become lost, like negotiating a freeway without a map or GPS. The solution is variety. Notice how I just chose to use a four-word sentence after a long sentence to add punch to my writing. The occasional very short sentence (VSS), or partial sentence, of three to five words can add

punch to a series of longer flowing sentences to make the reader sit up and take notice.

Allowing students to use sentence fragments in writing is controversial among teachers. Generally speaking, we want our students to understand and use complete sentences, particularly in formal writing. Sometimes, however, a fragment can be powerful enough to stand alone and add rhythm and interest to the sound of the text, most commonly in narrative writing. I don't discourage students from using an occasional fragment for effect, as long as they are aware that it's a fragment and are using it deliberately. Why should we prohibit our students from using a structure that they see in published writing all the time (Christensen & Christensen, 1978)? And that includes sentences beginning with conjunctions like *and* and *but,* which Francis Christensen and Bonniejean Christensen have found occur in almost 1 out of 10 sentences in published writing!

Writers put groups of words together in sentences and groups of sentences together in paragraphs. It may be argued that paragraphing is not really part of the writer's craft. But since I'm talking about crafting as building words into phrases and sentences, it seems logical to extend this construction one level higher. In the past, many teachers have treated paragraphing as a revision or editing tool—something writers do to a block of text *after* writing. Instead, I'd like to make a case for paragraphing as a drafting tool. I would like students to think in meaningful chunks of text, as an organizer for themselves as well as for their readers.

Expository writing tends to be easier to paragraph than narrative writing, because we start a new paragraph with each new subtopic (see Chapter 5). Paragraphing gets trickier in narrative writing, in which paragraphing is quite arbitrary and often becomes a matter of style. (Think of James Joyce, for example, who used few paragraphs at all.) However, most of our students need a little help to get started, and **The Five Ps of Paragraphing** offers them a guide for deciding when to start a new paragraph. I still believe that paragraphing is one of those developmental skills that students grow into as they become more sophisticated writers, but we need to give them something to grow into. Expecting correct paragraphing from fourth graders might be setting the bar too high, but that doesn't mean we can't introduce the concept and expect some effort at experimentation. Certainly, grade 4 students should be able to start a new paragraph with each new speaker, and by sixth grade, most students should have a strong sense of how to break up their text into comprehensible chunks. I generally tell young writers, "When in doubt, start a new paragraph. If it feels like there should be a break in the narrative, it's probably a good time to start a new paragraph." In school and on tests, students are more likely to get credit for attempting a paragraph than to get criticized for doing it incorrectly.

Our classrooms and libraries are bursting with books that can be used as mentor texts for teaching and modeling writer's craft. I believe we need to read every book at least twice: first as readers, for meaning, and the second time as writers, to analyze—and perhaps apply—the techniques the writer has used. Just because our students are in intermediate grades doesn't mean we should abandon the picture book! I use and reuse picture books like Ralph Fletcher's (1997) *Twilight Comes Twice*, David Wisniewski's (1998) *The Secret Knowledge of Grown-Ups*, Steven Layne's (2003) *My Brother Dan's Delicious*, and Jeron Ashford Frame's (2003) *Yesterday I Had the Blues*. Titles like these are geared to upper grade students, offering them much to learn and enjoy as readers as well as writers. As Regie Routman (2005) says, "Your students learn about sentences and paragraphs not by studying them in isolation, but through reading widely, hearing good literature read aloud and writing for audiences and purpose that matter" (p. 154).

Good literacy instruction involves explicit teaching, modeling, and practice in the context of connected reading and writing. It's not about worksheets and exercises in isolation. Students need freedom to write about ideas that really matter to them, but they need good teaching to help them master the words, sentences, and paragraphs that will help them convey those ideas most artfully to a reader. Teaching students to craft their ideas effectively is one of the most exciting and rewarding parts of the writing workshop. Using interesting words, unusual comparisons, figurative language, and varied sentences is sort of like pinning a diamond brooch to an elegant gown: It adds a little bling.

Vivid Verbs Bring Writing to Life

Verbs matter. Of all the parts of speech, verbs do the most to invigorate writing. Insipid verbs, such as *go*, *say*, and *take*, usually require an adverb to let the reader know just how that verb was carried out. But when a writer uses a more vivid and precise verb, such as *stroll*, *murmur*, or *devour*, the reader gets a clear picture of the action. In this lesson, students hunt for vivid verbs in a mentor text, practice replacing adverb–verb phrases, and revise their own writing with vivid verbs.

Learning Goal: Students will be able to identify and use vigorous verbs in their writing.

Trait: Word choice

Introduction: Review with the students what a verb is and what function it serves in a sentence.

Verbs may very well be the most important kind of word we use in writing! Remember that verbs convey an action (as in <u>run</u> or <u>talk</u>) or a state of being (like <u>is</u> and <u>were</u>). Every sentence must have a verb, and as a rule, the stronger the verbs, the more energized the sentences—and the writing overall—will be. In this lesson, you will learn how to use vivid verbs to liven up your writing.

Instruction: Share with the students the following list of verbs:

- went   • ate
- moved   • looked
- spoke

These verbs are pretty dull. They usually need a modifier attached to them to let the reader know just how the action was done. A sentence like "Jim spoke to his mother" doesn't tell the reader much about how Jim felt or what he meant. When writers use dull words, they often have to add a word like <u>slowly</u> or <u>loudly</u> to make the action clear to a reader. But, it would be a lot better if we just used a more vivid verb! Let's think about how we can brighten up these dull phrases with vivid verbs.

Display the following list and invite students to brainstorm vivid verbs to replace each two-word phrase:

- went slowly   • talked loudly
- moved quickly   • ate hungrily
- spoke softly

You may want to use a "carousel" technique, as described in **Say It With a Simile** (see page 152), to brainstorm replacement verbs for the verb–adverb phrases.

Guided Practice: Figure 7.2 contains an excerpt from the novel *The Countess and Me* by Paul Kropp (2002). The reproducible that follows this minilesson is an adaptation of that excerpt, with several strong verbs replaced by mundane verbs. Provide students with a copy of the adapted version of the excerpt. Have them work in pairs to replace each of the underlined verbs with a more powerful one. After completing the task, the students may be interested in comparing their words with the author's original text in Figure 7.2. Reinforce that this is not an exercise in right and wrong or trying to match the author's words; students may actually prefer some of their own word choices. In writing, every word is debatable.

Independent Application: Have students revise a piece of their own writing by replacing at least two dull verbs with more vivid verbs. They can also highlight any adverbs in a piece and consider whether to replace or delete them.

FIGURE 7.2. Excerpt From *The Countess and Me* With Vivid Verbs Underlined

I wasn't in my right mind when I <u>stormed</u> out of the house. I was so crazy mad that I didn't have a plan or strategy. It was Mordock's idea—break in, steal something and <u>terrorize</u> an old lady.

I <u>scribbled</u> some lame excuse to my mother, then took off for Cullen's house. I <u>dashed</u> over to the east side, <u>snuck</u> along the back and tried the patio door. Locked. To one side was a basement window, half-open already. I took my house key and <u>sliced</u> the screen, then pushed the screen up and slid out the window. Easy as pie.

Note. From The Countess and Me, by P. Kropp, 2002, Markham, ON, Canada: Fitzhenry & Whiteside, p. 118.

Excerpt from *The Countess and Me* With Strong Verbs Replaced

I wasn't in my right mind when I <u>went</u> out of the house. I was so crazy mad that I didn't have a plan or strategy. It was Mordock's idea—break in, steal something and <u>scare</u> an old lady.

I <u>wrote</u> some lame excuse to my mother, then took off for Cullen's house. I <u>walked</u> over to the east side, <u>went</u> along the back and tried the patio door. Locked. To one side was a basement window, half-open already. I took my house key and <u>cut</u> the screen, then pushed the screen up and slid out the window. Easy as pie.

Note. Adapted from *The Countess and Me,* by P. Kropp, 2002, Markham, ON, Canada: Fitzhenry & Whiteside, p. 118.
From *Marvelous Minilessons for Teaching Intermediate Writing, Grades 4–6* by Lori Jamison Rog. © 2011 International Reading Association.
May be copied for classroom use.

The Magic of Three

"I came, I saw, I conquered," said Julius Caesar (albeit in Latin), at least according to Plutarch. What makes this statement so memorable? There is something magical about putting parallel ideas together in threes. Linguists call it a tricolon. We call it the magic of three. In this lesson, students will practice grouping words and phrases in threes to add rhythm and cadence to their writing.

Learning Goal: Students will be able to put words, phrases, and ideas in groups of three for more effective writing.

Traits: Word choice, sentence fluency

Introduction: Present some famous examples of tricolons, such as the following:

- "Tell me and I forget. Teach me and I remember. Involve me and I learn." (Benjamin Franklin)
- "Life, Liberty and the pursuit of Happiness" (U.S. Declaration of Independence)
- "Peace, order and good government" (Canadian Constitution Act of 1867)
- "*Liberté, egalité, fraternité*" (national motto of France)
- "A happy life is one spent in learning, earning, and yearning." (Lillian Gish, American actress)
- "Government of the people, by the people, for the people." (Abraham Lincoln)

Tell students that each of these quotes is an example of the magic of three. Writers and speakers sometimes put three words or ideas together to make writing sound more musical and to pack more emotional punch. Tell students that in this lesson they will be practicing the magic of three to make their writing sound more interesting and rhythmical.

Instruction: Revisit the magic of three quotations and have students deconstruct the tricolon in each. Note that, in most cases, each of the three parts is the same length and structure: three nouns, three verbs, or three phrases or clauses. (Also note that there is a comma between each of the items in the group of three unless it is three sentences, in which case there is a period after each, of course.) You will need to decide whether you are going to teach the optional series comma (before *and* in lists of three or more items).

Date

_____

Observations

_____
_____
_____
_____
_____
_____
_____
_____
_____

Notes for Future Instruction

_____
_____
_____
_____
_____
_____
_____
_____
_____
_____
_____
_____

FIGURE 7.3. The "Magic of Three" Framework for Shared Writing

Three nouns: _____, _____, and _____ swam by us in the aquarium.

Three verbs: I was _____, _____, and _____ on the trampoline.

Three parallel phrases: At school, it's important to

_____,

_____, and

_____.

_____

    Display each of the sentence frames shown in Figure 7.3 one at a time. Have students turn and talk to a partner about possible words to complete each sentence. Talk about using words and phrases that go together and sound good to the ear. Use student contributions to complete each sentence.

Guided Practice: Provide students with their own copies of the "Song of the Seasons" framework (see the reproducible that follows this minilesson) and have them work individually or in pairs to complete the framework using the magic of three technique.

Independent Application: Students should highlight an example of the magic of three in their own writing or revise a piece to incorporate it.

The "Magic of Three" Framework
for "Song of the Seasons"

In the spring, _____,

_____, and

_____.

In the summer, _____,

_____, and

_____.

In the fall, _____,

_____, and

_____.

In the winter, _____,

_____, and

_____.

NOTES

Date

_____

Observations

_____
_____
_____
_____
_____
_____
_____
_____
_____

Notes for Future Instruction

_____
_____
_____
_____
_____
_____
_____
_____
_____
_____
_____
_____

Say It With a Simile

The simile must be the most popular comparison device ever created. There are as many similes in common use as there are sweaty socks in your school's lost-and-found box. Unique similes make writing more interesting and help readers perceive ideas in new ways. This minilesson uses *As: A Surfeit of Similes* by Norton Juster (1989), a lively read-aloud packed with similes in rhyming text. In this lesson, students will practice generating similes in groups as they "carousel" from one comparison to another.

Learning Goal: Students will be able to use fresh and original similes to make their writing more descriptive.

Traits: Ideas, word choice

Introduction: Provide students with a list of common similes or use some examples from Juster's (1989) *As: A Surfeit of Similes*, such as "As fair as a lily, as empty as air, as fresh as a daisy, as cross as a bear" or "As flat as a pancake, as warm as your socks, as short as bad tempers, as constant as clocks" (n.p.).

Ask students to turn and talk about what all of these phrases have in common. Tell them that the literary term for this kind of phrase is *simile*. (Here's a mnemonic that's also a simile: *Simile* is spelled like *smile* with an extra *i*.) Together, construct a definition for a simile, such as a writing technique that compares two ideas by using *like* or *as*. Tell them that in this lesson they will be learning how to use similes to make their writing more interesting, clear, and powerful.

Instruction: Talk with the students about why writers use similes. Discuss some of the similes from Juster's book and invite students to suggest some similes that they know. Compare similes that are fresh and original with those that have been used so much that they're a little tired, such as "dark as night" or "shines like silver." Discuss why Juster made the choices he did, for example, comparing *air* and *empty*, or *short* and *bad tempers*. Invite students to come up with alternatives for "as empty as…" or "as short as…."

Similes can be used to bring a fresh point of view about an object or idea, to make a difficult or unfamiliar idea more clear, or simply to help paint a picture in the reader's mind. That's why good writers don't use old and tired similes that everyone has already heard; good writers create fresh and original similes to offer a new way of thinking to their readers.

Guided Practice: Students will practice writing similes in groups using carousel brainstorming. On six to eight pieces of chart paper, write part of a simile at the top of each page, such as the following:

- as soft as
- as bright as
- as strong as
- as loud as
- as dirty as
- as sparkly as
- as tiny as
- as scratchy as

Post the chart papers around the room at an appropriate height for students to write on them.

Divide the students into groups of three or four and place each group at a different chart. Assign one person in each group to be the writer; the rest will be the brainstormers. Time the students for about three minutes. (The timing is arbitrary; observe the students to decide when to ring the bell.) During that time, the groups will brainstorm as many words as they can to complete the similes on their charts. When the time is up, each group cycles to the next chart in carousel fashion, with three minutes to add to what the previous group has written on the chart. Continue until each group has visited three or four charts. (If you allow more than that, then the energy will start to wane.) I like to use the carousel approach because it gives students an opportunity to get up and move. However, an alternative technique is "brainwriting," in which the students stay in place and the paper cycles from one group to the next.

When each group has had an opportunity to contribute to at least three or four charts, make one last carousel. Have the groups look at a chart they have not contributed to and discuss which they think are the most effective similes on the chart. Invite each group to read the three most creative similes on the chart in front of them. Talk with the students about what makes one simile more effective than another, such as fresh and original ideas, clear comparisons that make sense, and vivid images with strong word choices.

Independent Application: In writing workshop, have students revise a piece of writing in their writing folders to insert at least one simile.

Pop in a Popper

Poppers are appositives or other short phrases that writers pop into a sentence to elaborate on another word or idea. The rest of the sentence is intact, whether the appositive is popped in or out. In most cases, the popper is separated from the rest of the sentence with commas, although it is sometimes separated with dashes. In this lesson, students will practice popping poppers into their sentences to add description and flair.

Learning Goal: Students will be able to embed descriptive phrases (poppers) into sentences, with appropriate punctuation, to enhance or clarify nouns.

Traits: Ideas, word choice

Introduction: Link this lesson to students' prior knowledge about elaborating on nouns using adjectives. In English, we generally insert adjectives before a noun, but this lesson will focus on embedding descriptive phrases after nouns. Display the collection of sentences in Figure 7.4 and highlight the popper in each.

You're getting so good at putting describing words <u>before</u> a noun, such as "the green hat" or "a huge monster." However, sometimes we add a group of words <u>after</u> the noun to describe or clarify it. "The world's biggest football fan" tells something about my brother and why he paints his face, and "which was the coldest on record" describes the winter. You'll notice that each of the sentences is complete without the extra group of words, but when we pop those phrases into the sentences, the added phrases elaborate on the nouns and make the sentences more meaningful. That's why we call these phrases <u>poppers</u>. A popper is a group of words that are popped into a sentence to tell more about a noun.

FIGURE 7.4. Sentences With Poppers

- My brother, the world's biggest football fan, goes to games with his face painted in the team colors.

- Last winter, which was the coldest on record, our power went out for three days.

- Harry Potter, about a boy with magical powers, has become one of the best-selling series of all time.

Instruction: Invite students to turn and talk about what they know about poppers. They may also notice that the popper is separated from the rest of the sentence with commas. (Sometimes appositives are separated from the sentence by dashes instead.) They might observe that the popper may start with "which/who" or "is/was," or that phrase may be inferred. Reinforce that the sentence is already intact without the popper; it is popped into the sentence for elaboration or clarification.

Display some examples from literature, such as the following, and invite the students to locate the poppers:

> Keith, the boy in the rumpled shorts and shirt, did not know he was being watched as he entered room 215 of the Mountain View Inn. (from *The Mouse and the Motorcycle* by Beverly Cleary, 1965/2000, p. 11)
>
> Avon, a rather small snail, read a book every day. (from *The End of the Beginning* by Avi, 2004, p. 11)
>
> The massive thighs which emerged from out of the smock were encased in a pair of extraordinary breeches, bottle-green in colour and made of coarse twill. (from *Matilda* by Roald Dahl, 1988, p. 83)

Use an interactive writing approach to add poppers to the following sentence:

> Scrabble is enjoyed by kids of all ages.

Guided Practice: Display the sentences in the reproducible that follows this minilesson and have students work in pairs to pop in poppers in four or five sentences of their choice.

Independent Application: Have students revise a piece of writing in their writing folders by popping in at least one popper phrase.

Date

_____

Observations

_____

_____

_____

_____

_____

_____

_____

_____

_____

_____

_____

_____

Notes for Future Instruction

_____

_____

_____

_____

_____

_____

_____

_____

_____

_____

_____

_____

_____

Pop in a Popper

- Wayne Gretzky once scored five goals in one game!

- The kangaroo is native to Australia.

- Mr. Smith repaired our broken water pipe.

- J.K. Rowling wrote the Harry Potter series.

- I got these boots at Southland Mall.

- Denver is the home of the Denver Broncos.

- My car was damaged in an accident.

- The insect crawled along the floor.

- Jennifer's bedroom is full of clothes and collections.

Three-Sentence Stories

Sentence variety is pretty easy when you remember that there are really only four basic kinds of sentences: declarative, interrogative, imperative, and exclamatory. For students in the intermediate grades, it's probably easiest to name them statement, question, command, and exclamation. The command is the trickiest structure (with its implicit subject), so you might want to start with "three-sentence stories." Steven Layne's (2003) book *My Brother Dan's Delicious* is a model for many types of sentences, punctuation, and grammatical constructions.

Learning Goal: Students will be able to incorporate all three (or four) sentence types in a piece of writing.

Traits: Ideas, sentence fluency

Introduction: Review what students already know about sentences: They need a subject and a predicate, and they start with a capital and end with a piece of punctuation. I like to tell students that a sentence is a bit like a movie, in that just as a movie requires characters (who) and action (what), a sentence also requires a who and a what. Those are the things that sentences have in common. Today, the students are going to practice using different types of sentences in their writing.

Instruction: Display one of the excerpts from *My Brother Dan's Delicious* (see Figure 7.5), in which young Joey tries to convince an imaginary monster to eat his brother instead.

FIGURE 7.5. Excerpts From *My Brother Dan's Delicious*

Excerpt 1

Are there any monsters about? If there are, I just want you to know, my brother Dan's *delicious!* Yes, indeedy-do. He's one ultratasty guy.

Excerpt 2

Do I hear the sounds of stomach growling coming from behind that basement door? Well, just you *stay put!*

My brother Dan will be home soon; my brother Dan's *delicious!*

Note. From *My Brother Dan's Delicious*, by S.L. Layne, 2003, Gretna, LA: Pelican, n.p.

NOTES

Date

_____

Observations

_____
_____
_____
_____
_____
_____
_____
_____
_____

Notes for Future Instruction

_____
_____
_____
_____
_____
_____
_____
_____
_____
_____
_____

Invite students to turn and talk with a partner about the excerpt. How many sentences are there? What do they have in common? How are they different? Guide students to develop a name and definition for the four types of sentences: a question, a statement, a command, and an exclamation. If students are unfamiliar with these structures, you may want to construct an anchor chart as in Figure 7.6.

We're going to practice using different kinds of sentences by telling a story using only one statement, one question, and one exclamation. For example, I've just learned that I won the lottery. I might say, "Yippee, I won a million dollars! What will I do with all that money? I really should share it with my students." Now, you try. With your partner, create a three-sentence story about your bike being stolen from the schoolyard. Use only one statement, one question, and one exclamation, but they can be in any order.

FIGURE 7.6. Anchor Chart for Sentence Types

Sentence Type	Definition	Punctuation or Grammar Used	Example[a]
Statement (declarative)	• Most common type of sentence • Gives information or states a fact • Does not require an answer or response from the reader	• Period	"He's one ultratasty guy."
Question (interrogative)	• Asks a question • Requires an answer from the reader	• Question mark • Generally starts with *who, what, when, where, why,* or *how*	"Are there any monsters about?"
Exclamation	• Expressed with force or excitement	• Exclamation mark	"If there are, I just want you to know, my brother Dan's *delicious!*"
Command (imperative)	• Asks or tells someone to do something	• May have a period or exclamation mark, depending on forcefulness • Subject usually not stated and understood to be "you"	"Well, just you *stay put!*"

[a]From *My Brother Dan's Delicious*, by S.L. Layne, 2003, Gretna, LA: Pelican, n.p.

You may want to give your students more opportunities for oral-language practice before committing their ideas to paper. Provide them with scenarios such as school is dismissed early for a fire alarm, you scored a goal in the big game, or you just saw an amazing movie.

Guided Practice: Have the students repeat the three-sentence story activity in writing by using the reproducible that follows this minilesson. You may want to have them choose any three of the prompts provided. (If your students are ready to include imperative sentences, ask them to write four-sentence stories.)

Independent Application: Have students choose one of the drafts in their writing folders. Tell them to use a yellow highlighter to highlight any questions in the draft and a green highlighter for any exclamations. They should then revise by adding another question and another exclamation and highlight their revisions in orange.

NOTES

Date

Observations

Notes for Future Instruction

Three-Sentence Story Prompts

- Your parents don't think you need an allowance. Convince them you do.

- You just ate the worst meal in the world. Describe it.

- You saw the most unusual animal. Describe it.

- You didn't get your homework done and you don't want the teacher to know. Tell a friend.

- You just heard a hilarious joke. Tell it.

- You're so embarrassed/angry/disappointed because....

Flip the Sentence

Any piece of writing can sound dull and choppy when sentence after sentence begins the same way and has the same structure. One writer's trick for varying sentences is to change the order of the words: Flip a prepositional phrase from the end of the sentence to the beginning or flip two clauses. In this lesson, students learn to identify sentence chunks (prepositional phrases or subordinate clauses) and experiment with flipping their order. This is also an opportunity to teach students about using commas to separate a phrase or clause from the rest of the sentence.

Learning Goal: Students will be able to change the order of words in a sentence correctly and effectively to provide sentence variety.

Traits: Word choice, sentence fluency, conventions

Introduction: Display a collection of sentences, such as in Figure 7.7. Have the students turn and talk about the similarities and differences they notice in each pair of sentences.

Did you notice that both sentences in each pair say the same thing, but the order of the words is changed? In the second sentence, we simply flipped a group of words from the end of the sentence to the beginning. Today, you're going to learn about chunking and flipping sentence parts to make your writing sound more interesting.

FIGURE 7.7. Sentence Pairs for Flip the Sentence

- We had ice cream for dessert after dinner.
- For dessert, we had ice cream after dinner.

- There was a mysterious gift in the middle of the room.
- In the middle of the room, there was a mysterious gift.

- I need to take an umbrella in case it rains.
- In case it rains, I need to take an umbrella.

Date

Observations

Notes for Future Instruction

Date

_____
_____

Observations

_____
_____
_____
_____
_____
_____
_____
_____
_____
_____

Notes for Future Instruction

_____
_____
_____
_____
_____
_____
_____
_____
_____
_____
_____

Instruction: Present this excerpt from David Wisniewski's (1998) *The Secret Knowledge of Grown-Ups* (or choose an example of your own):

> Just like carrot seeds become carrots and bean seeds become beans, fingernail scraps become fingers. After growing under your bed or between the sofa pillows for about three months, the new fingers leave their nests and go crawling around the house.
>
> At first, this isn't too much of a problem. With their dimpled knuckles and sunny dispositions, the baby fingers are actually kind of cute. But as they get older, the fingers start behaving badly. (n.p.)

With the students, analyze these five sentences. First, divide each sentence into chunks by separating the prepositional phrase from the kernel of the sentence. Take note of the way phrases like "just like carrot seeds become carrots," "at first," and "after growing under your bed or between the sofa pillows for about three months" tell when or how.

You may want to use this opportunity to identify prepositions as a part of speech. Note the structure of the word *preposition*; prepositions tell you the *position* of the rest of the sentence—in time or space. Together, try chunking and flipping each sentence. Each sentence variation should still be grammatically correct, but some variations will sound better than others. Here's a note on punctuation: If the prepositional phrase or subordinate clause is at the beginning of the sentence, it is *usually* separated from the rest of the sentence with a comma.

Not every sentence lends itself to flipping. For example, "Fingernail scraps become fingers just like carrot seeds become carrots and bean seeds become beans" just doesn't have the same ring as the original. Read the sentence to yourself and listen to its rhythm. Trust your ears and your head! If you want to emphasize one part of the sentence over another, the most important part should probably go first. Your ears will also let you know whether there should be a comma separating the two parts of the sentence.

If a group of sentences sounds plodding to the ear, take a closer look. Do they all have the same subject–verb structure? Chunking and flipping just one or two sentences might be the solution to making your text sound more interesting and rhythmical.

Guided Practice: The reproducible that follows this minilesson contains a paragraph adapted from the novel *The Crash* by Paul Kropp (2005) to create a series of sentences that all have the same subject–predicate format. Even though this is quite an exciting bit of text in the actual novel

FIGURE 7.8. Original Excerpt From *The Crash*

Up in front, Mrs. D was pumping the brake pedal like crazy....

I gripped the handrail as hard as I could while the bus slid and bumped across the road and back again. Then there was the scream of metal crunching metal. We hit the metal guard rail beside the road. If we were in a car, the rail would have bounced us back.

But we were in a school bus. We smashed over the guard rail and the bus tipped sideways....

Then we began sliding. The school bus was tipped on its right side and we were sliding down the hill....

The thumps began. The school bus would hit something—a bush or a rock—and the whole bus would shake. For a few seconds, it seemed like we were picking up speed. Then we smashed into something big. Wham! The whole bus flipped around, front to back.

And then it was quiet.

After the awful noise of crashing metal and bouncing down the hill, the silence was good. There was only the hiss of the bus now. For a few seconds, it had all stopped.

Note. From *The Crash*, by P. Kropp, 2005, Toronto, ON, Canada: High Interest, pp. 12, 14–15.

(see Figure 7.8), the modified version sounds slow and plodding because of the sluggish sentence structures. Have students work with a partner to choose two or three of the sentences in the handout to chunk and flip. (Students may want to compare their ideas to the actual text from the book. This is not intended to be a matching game, but rather students should examine the way a professional author crafts sentences.)

Independent Application: Have students choose a piece of writing from their writing folders to revise by flipping one or two sentences.

Modified Excerpt From *The Crash*

Mrs. D was pumping the brake pedal like crazy up in front. I gripped the handrail as hard as I could while the bus slid and bumped across the snow. We hit a metal guard rail beside the road. It seemed like we were picking up speed for a few seconds. We smashed into something big all of a sudden. Then it was quiet. The silence was good after the awful noise of crashing metal and bouncing down the hill. There was only the hiss of the bus now. Everything stopped at last.

Note. Original excerpt from *The Crash*, by P. Kropp, Toronto, ON, Canada: High Interest, pp. 12, 14–15.
From *Marvelous Minilessons for Teaching Intermediate Writing, Grades 4–6* by Lori Jamison Rog. © 2011 International Reading Association. May be copied for classroom use.

The Five Ps of Paragraphing

Moving from words to sentences to paragraphs is a challenge for many of our intermediate-grade writers. Most of them are beginning to paragraph in their expository writing by simply starting a new paragraph with each new subtopic. However, paragraphing gets trickier with narrative writing. In this lesson, we teach students a rule of thumb to start a new paragraph each time there is a change in the five Ps of paragraphing:

- person speaking
- point in time
- place
- plot direction
- point of view

Learning Goal: Students will be able to experiment with paragraphing a narrative text and justify their choices of paragraph breaks.

Traits: Organization, conventions

Introduction: Talk to the students about what they already know about paragraphing and why we have paragraphs. Most intermediate students will be aware of indentation as a paragraph marker; if not, it would be helpful to examine a page from any classroom novel or textbook.

Paragraphs are a tool for breaking up large chunks of text into manageable pieces for a reader. A change in paragraphs gives the reader some breathing space and signals that there is some sort of change in a story. In nonfiction, we start a new paragraph with each new topic or subtopic, but it's a little harder to decide when to start a new paragraph in narrative writing. In this lesson, you're going to learn some tricks to help you decide when to start a new paragraph in your writing.

Instruction: Choose any narrative text sample that is broken into several paragraphs. You may want to have students pull out a novel from their desks, open it to any page, and see if they can come up with any generalizations about how the writer has decided to start new paragraphs.

This may also be a good time to dispel any misconceptions about paragraphs. There are no rules for how many sentences to put in a paragraph or how many paragraphs belong in an essay (contrary to popular belief). Paragraphing can vary considerably from one text to another. Newspaper articles, for example, have many short paragraphs,

Observations

Notes for Future Instruction

often comprising only one long sentence each. Novels are likely to have some long descriptive paragraphs full of many flowing sentences as well as short paragraphs of dialogue. The only rule is that there is *no* rule about how many or what kinds of sentences belong in a paragraph.

Your students may already know that a new paragraph starts whenever a new person speaks. They may also be able to identify changes in time, place, plot direction, or point of view in a sample text. Although there are no hard-and-fast rules for when to start a new paragraph in a story, the five Ps offer some general guidelines:

- *Person speaking:* Every time a new character speaks, we start a new paragraph, even if the previous speaker has only said one word of dialogue.
- *Point in time:* Phrases like "later that night" or "the next day" are signals. When the time changes, so does the paragraph.
- *Place:* If the action moves from one location to another, it's a good time to change the paragraph.
- *Plot direction:* Often a change in the action signals a new paragraph.
- *Point of view:* If the narrative has been focusing on one character and shifts to another, change the paragraph.

Guided Practice: Have students mark up the reproducible at the end of this lesson, which is a modified excerpt from the novel *Shooting the Rapids* by Paul Kropp (2006), to add paragraph breaks. (You may want to teach the editing symbol for "start a new paragraph" [¶].) Working in pairs, they can discuss the reasons for their paragraph choices. The original text is provided in Figure 7.9. Be sure to take time to discuss the author's and students' paragraphing choices as a group, so the students learn to become purposeful in their writing and articulate their decisions.

Independent Application: Writers use paragraphs to break up a long piece of text for readers and for themselves. That's why writers *think* in paragraphs. They don't go back into a block of text to chunk it after they've drafted. We want students to use paragraphing as a drafting tool, not just an editing tool. You may want to have students edit a piece of their own writing for paragraphs, but you should establish the expectation that students will experiment with paragraphing while drafting and be able to justify their decisions about where paragraphs were changed.

FIGURE 7.9. Original Excerpt From *Shooting the Rapids*

We both paddled like crazy. In a minute, we had the canoe under control, but that minute cost us. We were at the start of the rapids.

"It's too late. We can't get to shore!" Timmy yelled.

That was the truth. We were in the middle of the river, with rock ledges on both sides. Up ahead, the water swirled over rocks. Spray and foam shot up when the water hit a rock. And we were moving fast.

"Okay, we can do this," I shouted to Timmy. I wasn't sure he could hear me. The river sounded like thunder as it hit the rocks. "You tell me what's coming. I'll steer."…

The water pushed us like a speedboat. Around us, the water crashed into rocks at the shore. Spray shot up and fell down on us.

I thought, *this is like a fun park*. But this was not a fun park ride, this was real. Boats crash in whitewater. People get thrown by whitewater. People die in whitewater. We had a chance—but only a chance—of coming out alive.

Note. From *Shooting the Rapids*, by P. Kropp, 2006, Toronto, ON, Canada: High Interest, pp. 55, 57.

Excerpt From *Shooting the Rapids* With Paragraph Breaks Removed

We both paddled like crazy. In a minute, we had the canoe under control, but that minute cost us. We were at the start of the rapids. "It's too late. We can't get to shore!" Timmy yelled. That was the truth. We were in the middle of the river, with rock ledges on both sides. Up ahead, the water swirled over rocks. Spray and foam shot up when the water hit a rock. And we were moving fast. "Okay, we can do this," I shouted to Timmy. I wasn't sure he could hear me. The river sounded like thunder as it hit the rocks. "You tell me what's coming. I'll steer."… The water pushed us like a speedboat. Around us, the water crashed into rocks at the shore. Spray shot up and fell down on us. I thought, this is like a fun park. But this was not a fun park ride, this was real. Boats crash in whitewater. People get thrown by whitewater. People die in whitewater. We had a chance—but only a chance—of coming out alive.

Note. Adapted from *Shooting the Rapids*, by P. Kropp, Toronto, ON, Canada: High Interest, 2006, pp. 55, 57.
From *Marvelous Minilessons for Teaching Intermediate Writing, Grades 4–6* by Lori Jamison Rog. © 2011 International Reading Association.
May be copied for classroom use.

CHAPTER 8

Success on the Test

Here's your task: You must plan, draft, revise, and edit a piece of writing. The topic may or may not have any relevance to you. By the way, you have 60 minutes to do all of this. Don't forget that you will be judged on how well you do. It certainly will have an influence on your report card—and may have an impact on whether you pass or fail your grade.

In more and more places, students are being confronted with this testing scenario. The prompts, the times, and the stakes will vary—but one thing is common: an artificially created situation in which students will be evaluated on how well they write. Many states, provinces, districts, and even countries now have some form of annual writing assessment similar to this. Even the Scholastic Aptitude Test added a writing component in 2005.

Research, good practice, and common sense tell us that the best test preparation is a good writing program (Langer, 2002). When teachers focus their energies on helping their students become effective, literate communicators, the students generally do well on tests. A solid literacy curriculum, well taught, with ongoing assessment and high expectations, is the best preparation for tests and for life. If students have had many opportunities to write on a wide variety of topics for a wide variety of audiences, they won't freeze when the test paper appears. When students have mastered a process for revising their writing, they will be better able to revise as they write during a testing situation. When students have a repertoire of planning tools up their sleeves, they will be better able to organize their thoughts on a writing task before putting pen to paper.

That said, we owe it to our students to ensure that they get credit on any test for what they know and can do. Even in wonderful writing workshop classrooms, we will find students who fail to measure up in a standardized testing situation. How often have we heard of students who blew the test because they've never written to a prompt before, or don't finish the writing because they've never encountered a time limit in their process? It's only fair to familiarize them with the test situation, so they can demonstrate their best work. This chapter offers five minilessons to support students in the types of writing they will encounter on tests as well as other areas of classroom writing (see Table 8.1 for an overview of the minilessons in this chapter).

TABLE 8.1. Success on the Test Minilessons at a Glance

Minilesson	Page	Trait(s)Addressed	Lesson Focus
The Umbrella Statement	175	Ideas, organization, sentence fluency	Writing a summary statement in response to a prompt
BIBB: Bring It Back to the Book!	179	Ideas	Adding support from the text
Sum It Up in a Summary	182	Ideas, organization, word choice, sentence fluency, conventions	Step-by-step process for writing a summary
Hook, Line, and Sinker	187	Ideas, organization	Writing an opener, middle, and closing in response to a prompt
Budgeting Your Time	191	Ideas, organization, voice, word choice, sentence fluency, conventions	Writing to a prompt within a time limit

It is both inappropriate and futile to allow the year's writing curriculum to be driven by testing. "Teaching to the test" undermines teaching and learning, not to mention the validity of the text itself (Volante, 2004). Furthermore, teaching to the test doesn't much help in writing. Repeated practice with released test items often forces students to focus on the prompts instead of the quality of their writing.

However, it is quite possible and appropriate to align the goals of the writing program with the standards and expectations of the test. Don't wait until testing time to familiarize yourself with the rubrics and integrate them into your classroom instruction and assessment. Ensure that the standards and expectations of the test are part of your writing curriculum. As Judith Langer (2002) suggests, integrating test preparation with the foundational curriculum leads to better test scores and better learning overall:

> Overall, effective schools seemed to focus on students' learning, using the tests to be certain that the skills and knowledge tested were being learned within the framework of improved language arts instruction, while the typical schools seemed to focus on the tests themselves, with raising test scores, rather than students' literacy learning, as the primary goal. (p. 23)

Unfortunately, many students have trouble transferring what they have learned as communicators to a writing-on-demand situation. Experts such as Janet Angelillo (2005) and Lucy Calkins and her colleagues (Calkins, Montgomery, & Santman, 1998) suggest treating test writing as a separate writing genre and integrating a brief unit on the unique challenges of test writing into the curriculum.

In many ways, test writing requires the same skills and strategies as other types of written communication: developing and shaping an idea, using words that paint pictures in the reader's mind, and conveying passion and commitment to the topic. Unfortunately, the passion and commitment part is a little tricky, mainly because students must write to an external prompt, usually within a limited time frame. We all know the reasons behind allowing students to choose their own topics: They're more motivated and engaged, more willing to revise and edit, and more likely to write with voice and feeling. However, it has been argued that writing to a prompt is an essential life skill. After all, how often do most of us as adults write without being prompted? All the time, actually. We drop an e-mail to a friend or associate, fill out an application or an order form, write a report on a student, or compose an entry for the school newsletter.

Some would argue that those are all examples of *prompted* writing. We write that report because we are required to do so; in truth, we probably wouldn't be doing it otherwise. Yet, I would argue that this type of writing is less about prompting and more about audience and purpose. We write a report on a student for an administrator or a special program (our audience) to better meet the educational needs of that student (our purpose). We write a newsletter to parents (our audience) to keep them informed about what's happening in the class (our purpose). When we think about a prompt in terms of the reader and the reason for writing, it usually makes it easier for us to put our thoughts into words on the page.

Prompts are a reality in test writing. Using the same prompt for all students is one means of leveling the playing field, so to speak, both for writing and for scoring. Some might say it's a way of ensuring that all writers are equally disadvantaged. One way to help students respond to external prompts is to teach them to identify their audience and purpose before they write, as in the minilesson **TAP Into Writing** (see page 38 in Chapter 3).

There are two main types of prompts used in writing assessments: responses to reading and open-ended topics. Reading response assessments are generally concerned with understanding and interpreting what was read. They tend to focus more on idea development, organization, and support from the text than the craft of writing. Three of the minilessons in this chapter are intended to help develop the kinds of skills students need in literature response, and Table 8.2 contains a list of sample prompts from familiar fairy tales that might be used for the minilessons in this chapter, as well as additional practice in writing effective responses to reading.

The first minilesson, **The Umbrella Statement**, provides students with practice in restating the prompt and creating an overview of the written response. Restating the prompt in the opening sentence helps clarify the

TABLE 8.2. Sample Fairy Tale Prompts for Practice

1. What could Little Red Riding Hood have done to prevent the problems she had?
2. What should the three bears do with Goldilocks? What would be an appropriate punishment?
3. Who do you think was the villain in *Jack and the Beanstalk*, Jack or the giant?
4. Which of the fairy tale characters would you choose to be friends with?
5. Which of the three pigs was most important to the story? Why do you think so?
6. How did the pea let people know the girl was a princess? What would be a better test?
7. Can you think of a nonviolent way for the third billy goat to get across the bridge?
8. What is the lesson we should learn from *Beauty and the Beast*? Do you agree with it?
9. What is meant when someone says you are "crying wolf"?
10. Why did the witch choose to take away the little mermaid's voice? Why was this the most difficult thing for the mermaid?
11. In *Rumpelstiltskin*, who is the villain and who is the hero?
12. How would the story of Cinderella be the same and different if Cinderella were a boy?
13. How did the character _____ change from beginning to end?
14. What is the lesson we can learn from _____? How can we apply this lesson to real life?
15. How are the characters _____ and _____ alike and different?
16. Compare the settings of _____ and _____.

question in the mind of the writer and guide and focus the response. It also indicates to the scorer that the writer has at least a basic understanding of what is asked, usually the foundational criteria for at least a basic score. The restatement of the prompt is then turned into a topic sentence—an umbrella over the supporting details to come. The umbrella statement is particularly important for prompts that require a response to literature. For open-ended prompts, scorers are generally looking for a more engaging hook, although students are usually advised to insert a direct reference to the prompt in the opening paragraph. **BIBB: Bring It Back to the Book!** uses an acronym developed by Adrienne Gear (2006), in her book *Reading Power: Teaching Students to Think While They Read*, to teach students to support their responses with evidence from the text.

Test writing is one of many academic situations that require intermediate students to write summaries. Robert Marzano and his colleagues (Marzano et al., 2001) have identified summarizing as one of the nine most important strategies for improving student achievement. Summarizing is also one of the four steps in the well-documented reciprocal teaching strategy (Palincsar & Brown, 1986). The reality is that our students are often *assigned* to write summaries but not always *taught* to write them. **Sum It Up in a Summary** provides a framework for summarizing a piece of literature.

The open-ended prompt is most often narrative, although it may be descriptive or persuasive, and often takes a form I call the "mad, sad, or glad" topic, such as "tell about one of the most exciting experiences in your life," "describe a problem you had and how you dealt with it," or "what do you think is the greatest invention in the world and why?" These writing assessments generally expect students to develop a topic with effective detail, word choice, fluency, and voice. **Hook, Line, and Sinker** offers students a graphic organizer for planning an open-ended response. This simple organizer teaches students to plan an engaging opening (hook), a well-crafted body (line), and a satisfying conclusion (sinker).

Real writers of all ages know that writing takes time. Good writing rarely, if ever, springs forth from the pen in perfect form. Some writing requires hours of meditation and planning before ever setting that pen to paper. Other writing demands revision after revision before it reaches its final form. Unfortunately, many test writers don't know this. They think developing writers can compose and craft a piece of writing in 45 or 60 or 90 minutes. Some enlightened test developers allow students as much time as they need, as long as they don't need any more than a school day. For most students, the challenge of writing on demand within a limited time frame is stressful at best and debilitating at worst. The final minilesson in this chapter, **Budgeting Your Time**, provides students with practice in planning, drafting, and correcting their writing within the time constraints of a test situation.

As I said earlier in this chapter, teaching test preparation will not make students better writers—and won't even guarantee better test scores. Good ongoing teaching of the writing process, from kindergarten on, is the best bet for strong test scores. A few lessons on test writing simply makes students more test-savvy and helps them get the most credit for what they know and can do. However, after years of coordinating writing assessments, developing large-scale reading assessments, and researching testing practices across the globe, I have some general observations about ways we can help students get the credit they deserve on writing tests:

1. *Mechanics do not matter as much as most people think.* In the majority of cases, spelling, punctuation, and grammatical errors significantly affect test scores only when they are so ineffective as to make reading difficult. Students should be encouraged to use a powerful word, even if they're not sure how to spell it, or a flowing sentence, even if they think the punctuation may be incorrect. Scorers are more inclined to give credit for risk-taking than to take marks away for occasional mistakes in conventions.

2. *Voice matters more than most people think.* On the test's rubric, "voice" may appear as "style," "tone," or "recognition of audience"—or it may not

appear at all. However, voice is what connects a piece of text to a reader, and unless the writing is being scored mechanically, there is likely to be a human reader on the other end of the piece. Encourage students to think of their writing as a letter to a reader.

3. *Pay attention to the prompt.* One of the first things scorers look for is whether the writing addresses the prompt. A respectful nod to the prompt at the outset allows students more freedom in writing later on.

4. *Paragraphs are powerful!* When in doubt, start a new paragraph. Students are more likely to get credit for just trying paragraphs than to get docked for paragraphing unnecessarily. (See the minilesson **The Five Ps of Paragraphing** on page 165 in Chapter 7.)

5. *Teach students to double-space their writing, both to allow space for revision and to make it easier to read.* There is no doubt that word-processed test writing looms in the near future, as computers become more accessible and scoring budgets more frugal. But as of this writing, most tests are still conducted on paper with human scorers. I have yet to see neat handwriting listed as a criterion on a test rubric, but the tired scorer who is on her 500th piece of writing is more likely to start with an open mind if that piece is written legibly. The scorer who is wavering between a 3 and a 4 might just be positively influenced by a piece that is clearly written and easy to read. Or, the opposite might happen if he or she has to struggle to make out the script. Encouraging students to double-space their writing won't turn scrawls into calligraphy, but allowing more white space can make even the sloppiest handwriting easier to navigate. In most cases, students can get more paper if they need it.

> ### Quick Tips for Students Responding to Writing Test Prompts
>
> - Refer directly to the prompt.
> - Think of your writing as a letter to a real person.
> - Take a chance on a wonderful word, even if you don't know how to spell it.
> - Paragraphs are powerful, so when in doubt, start a new one.
> - Double-space your writing, because it looks neater, and you can always get more paper if you need it.

Test writing is a reality of life for students and teachers. We've all heard stories of ways to trick the testers, skew the scoring, and distort the data. In the minilessons in this chapter, I hope to encourage raising test scores the old-fashioned way: with better writing.

The Umbrella Statement

An umbrella statement that restates the test prompt and summarizes the answer is particularly important for literature response assessments. Restating the prompt in the opening sentence of the response serves two important purposes: (1) helps the writer clarify what the question is about and organizes his or her response, and (2) indicates to the scorer that the writer has at least a basic understanding of what is asked. We call the opening statement the "umbrella," because it overarches the remaining details and prevents the writing from being drenched in random ideas—but perhaps I'm pushing the metaphor.

Using familiar topics or literature examples is a good way to practice restating the prompt. Any familiar literature example will do; for the purpose of this lesson, we'll use prompts from familiar fairy tales, as listed in Table 8.2 (page 172). Another useful resource is "The Better Answer Game" (Rickey, 2010), an interactive website that helps students practice using words in the prompt as part of the answer (www.netrover. com/~kingskid/Better_Answer/answer.html).

Learning Goal: Students will be able to provide an overview statement that restates the prompt and provides a general response.

Traits: Ideas, organization, sentence fluency

Introduction: Talk with the students about the importance of understanding what the question is asking. Remind them that an umbrella statement is like a topic sentence that organizes their own thinking and lets scorers know that they understand what the question is asking.

Whenever we need to respond to a question or prompt, the first step is to understand the question. We need to know what the question is asking in order to answer it! We also need to let our reader know that <u>we</u> know what we are being asked. That's why we start with a sentence that uses as many words from the prompt as possible. Then, we want to give a summary of our answer—kind of an umbrella over all the details to come. That's why we call it an <u>umbrella sentence</u>. Just as we use a topic sentence in research writing, an umbrella sentence summarizes the details that will come. Today, we're going to practice writing umbrella sentences using words from the prompt.

Instruction: Start with some easy questions to assess how well your students can answer a question using as many words as possible from the prompt:

• *What was the name of the girl who went into the three bears' house?*

The name of the girl who went into the three bears' house was Goldilocks.

Suggest to students that they avoid replacing nouns with pronouns in the umbrella sentence:

• *Who was Little Red Riding Hood going to visit?*

Little Red Riding Hood was going to visit her grandmother.

The only exception to the pronoun rule occurs when the prompt uses "you." The important thing is to remember to change "you" to "I":

• *Which character would you choose to have as a friend?*

I would choose....

Remember to change the verb tense, if necessary:

• *Why did Little Red Riding Hood <u>think</u> the wolf was her grandmother?*

Little Red Riding Hood *thought* the wolf was her grandmother, because the wolf was hiding under the covers and couldn't be seen clearly.

The task gets a little harder when the prompt does not take the form of a question:

• *Compare the characters of Goldilocks and Little Red Riding Hood.*

Goldilocks and Little Red Riding Hood are both little girls in fairy tales, but that's where the similarities end.

A test prompt will never be answered in just one sentence. Trust me, even if it looks like one sentence will do, scorers will always expect more. The first sentence is just the umbrella, and the rest of the response will give more information and support from the text.

Guided Practice: Share with students the umbrella statement checklist in the reproducible that follows this lesson. Have students turn and talk with a partner to discuss which of the three umbrella sentences are best for the prompt below:

Prompt: In the story *Jack and the Beanstalk*, do you think Jack was a villain or a hero?

Umbrella sentences:

1. I think Jack was the villain.

2. In the story *Jack and the Beanstalk*, I think Jack was a villain.

3. In the story *Jack and the Beanstalk*, I think Jack was a villain because he was the one who committed crimes against the giant.

With the group, discuss the reasons why the third example is the best choice. (It uses words from the prompt and gives a summary of the answer to come.)

Independent Application: Provide one or a choice of prompts from Table 8.2 for students to begin working on independently.

Quick Tips for Writing Umbrella Statements

- Avoid replacing nouns with pronouns (except to respond with "I" when the prompt asks about "you").

- Try to use as many words directly from the prompt as possible to send a message to the scorer that you know what you are being asked and help organize your thinking.

- Make a direct reference to the passage in the umbrella statement to send a message to the scorer that you've actually read the text you're being asked about.

- Change the verb tense if necessary.

- Watch for prompts that have two or more parts. Be sure to answer all of them.

- Always explain "why," even if the prompt doesn't ask you to.

Date

Observations

Notes for Future Instruction

Umbrella Statement Checklist

❑ Did you use as many words as possible from the prompt?

❑ Does your umbrella sentence show that you understand the prompt?

❑ Does the topic sentence give a summary of your answer?

❑ Does your topic sentence open the door to more elaboration in your response?

✄ -

Umbrella Statement Checklist

❑ Did you use as many words as possible from the prompt?

❑ Does your umbrella sentence show that you understand the prompt?

❑ Does the topic sentence give a summary of your answer?

❑ Does your topic sentence open the door to more elaboration in your response?

Marvelous Minilessons for Teaching Intermediate Writing, Grades 4–6 by Lori Jamison Rog. © 2011 International Reading Association. May be copied for classroom use.

BIBB: Bring It Back to the Book!

BIBB is an acronym for "bring it back to the book," a reminder to writers that they must back up their responses with direct examples and evidence from the reading (Gear, 2006). Offering supporting evidence is a key to higher scores on a literature-based writing assessment. This minilesson offers students practice in providing both general examples and direct quotes from the text to support their responses.

Learning Goal: Students will be able to cite evidence from the text to support their responses to a literature prompt.

Trait: Ideas

Introduction: Remind students that answering the question or responding to the prompt is only part of their job. The other part is to support their response with proof from the text. In this lesson, students will practice looking for evidence from the text. We use the acronym *BIBB* to remind us to "bring it back to the book."

Instruction: Tell students to look at the prompt from *Jack and the Beanstalk*: "Who do you think was the villain in *Jack and the Beanstalk*, Jack or the giant?" With the students, develop an umbrella statement, such as, "In the story *Jack and the Beanstalk*, I think Jack was a villain, because he committed all sorts of crimes against the giant."

Together, generate a list of evidence from the text to support the idea that Jack is really the villain. (Reread a version of the familiar tale if you think it is necessary.) Some ideas from the text might include

- Even at the beginning, Jack disobeyed his mother and traded the cow for a handful of beans instead of selling the cow for food.
- The giant was minding his own business, eating his dinner, when Jack snuck into his house and stole first a bag of gold coins, then a hen that laid golden eggs, and finally a magic harp.
- As the giant climbed down the beanstalk after him, Jack grabbed an ax and chopped down the beanstalk. The story says, "The giant fell to earth, hitting the ground so hard that it split, pulling the beanstalk down with him."

Model writing these ideas in a complete response and think-aloud, such as the following:

In the story *Jack and the Beanstalk*, I think Jack was the villain, because he committed all sorts of crimes against the giant.

Date

Observations

Notes for Future Instruction

N O T E S

Date

_____

_____

Observations

_____

_____

_____

_____

_____

_____

_____

_____

_____

Notes for Future Instruction

_____

_____

_____

_____

_____

_____

_____

_____

_____

_____

_____

_____

_____

There's our umbrella statement, which summarizes our response and names the text. Now, let's insert a sentence that supports our umbrella sentence.

> I don't think the giant did anything evil except try to protect his own property.

Here's our first example from the story.

> Right from the start, Jack disobeyed his mother by trading the cow for a handful of beans instead of for food.

Here's another example.

> It was Jack who broke into the giant's house, not the other way around. The giant was minding his own business, eating his dinner, when Jack snuck into his house and stole a bag of gold coins.

And here's a third example from the story.

> That wasn't even enough for Jack. He came back and stole a hen that laid golden eggs and then a magic harp. The giant was coming after Jack to get his own property back, and Jack chopped down the beanstalk.

Now we can add a direct quote right from the story.

> As the story says, "The giant fell to earth, hitting the ground so hard that it split, pulling the beanstalk down with him."

Next, I'm going to add a little extra thought of my own.

> Although in fairy tales we are supposed to think that all giants are evil and boys are heroes, I think Jack did more evil things than the giant did.

I summarized the main point to conclude.

Talk with the students about what makes this an effective response:

- An umbrella statement that restates the prompt and gives a summary of the answer
- Specific examples from the text, including a direct quote
- A little extra thought beyond the prompt
- A wrap-up sentence summarizing the main point

Guided Practice: Provide a prompt from the list in Table 8.2 (page 172) or choose one of your own. Have students work in pairs to construct a response, then use highlighters to underscore their evidence from the text. Suggest that they use two different colors, one for direct quotes from the text and another for references to the text.

Independent Application: Have students work independently on constructing a response to one of the prompts provided.

NOTES

Date

Observations

Notes for Future Instruction

Date

_____

_____

Observations

_____
_____
_____
_____
_____
_____
_____
_____
_____
_____
_____
_____
_____

Notes for Future Instruction

_____
_____
_____
_____
_____
_____
_____
_____
_____
_____
_____
_____
_____
_____
_____
_____

Sum It Up in a Summary

Students are called on to write summaries in many academic situations, of which test writing is only one. Yet, when asked to summarize, our students often write either too much or too little, or simply retell what was stated in the text. A summary "is a shortened version of an original text, stating the main ideas and important details of the text with the same text structure and order of the original" (Kissner, 2006, p. 8).

All in all, summarizing is a pretty demanding task for intermediate writers. First, they need to be able to analyze, prioritize, and synthesize the information that they have read. Then, they must restate, combine, organize, and paraphrase pieces of information in order to create a summary. Explicit teaching and plenty of guided practice are essential for helping students master this critical learning skill. In this minilesson, there is the added challenge of externally summarizing a piece of narrative text, which means changing the point of view from first to third person and changing the tense from past to present, as is commonly required of a literature summary. Depending on the skill level of the students, teachers may want to start with practicing with nonfiction texts.

Learning Goal: Students will be able to effectively summarize a piece of fiction or nonfiction reading.

Traits: Ideas, organization, word choice, sentence fluency, conventions

Introduction: By the intermediate grades, your students should have had some prior experience with summarizing, both formally and informally. Talk with them about different ways we summarize all the time.

Let's say you've just watched the weather report on television and your mom asks you what the weather's going to be like tomorrow. You don't repeat every word the weather forecaster said. You might say, "It's supposed to be hot and muggy in the morning, but there might be thunderstorms in the afternoon." That's a summary. It's a shortened version of the weather report, with just the main points. We all summarize all the time: when we tell someone about a book we're reading, about a game we played or a show we watched, or about a conversation we had with someone else. Summarizing is a short form of the whole story, with just the most important points.

Activate students' background knowledge by having them contribute their ideas of what a summary is and what they do when they summarize a story or other text in school. Distinguish between a retelling (listing every detail from the text in order) and a summary (a shortened version of the text, highlighting the main points and most important details in the order that they appeared in the text).

Provide students with a set of rules for summarizing (see Table 8.3). Think aloud as you model a process for marking up a text to summarize. A sample text that you may choose to use is provided in Figure 8.1, with "teacher talk" included in Figure 8.2. Note that when we summarize a text that is written in the first person, we change it to the third person; in other words, "I" becomes "he."

TABLE 8.3. Rules for Summarizing

- Take out information that's not important.
- Take out repeated information.
- Substitute category words for lists.
- Combine ideas or events that go together.
- Put ideas in your own words.

Note. Adapted from *A Handbook for Classroom Instruction That Works*, by R.J. Marzano, J.S. Norford, D.E. Paynter, D.J. Pickering, & B.B. Gaddy, 2001, Alexandria, VA: Association for Supervision and Curriculum Development, p. 60. (Adapted from "Learning to Learn: On Training Students to Learn From Texts," by A.L. Brown, J.C. Campione, & J.D. Day, 1981, *Educational Researcher*, 10(2), 14–21)

FIGURE 8.1. Text Sample for Summary Writing

Lost in the Woods

I was alive. It was morning and the dawn light had turned everything reddish-orange. When my heart stopped pounding, I realized that I was thirsty and hungry. Even worse, those berries I'd eaten the night before weren't sitting in my stomach too well. That's all I needed—to start throwing up again.

So I started off, my mouth dry and my stomach heaving. I had a full day of walking ahead of me and there were two people back at the crash site who were depending on me. I was determined to keep on going, no matter how queasy I felt.

I came across water two hours later. It was only a small stream, but as far as I was concerned, it was the best water I'd ever tasted.

By afternoon, I was so starved I would have eaten my shoes. I decided to risk some of the berries again, despite what they did to my stomach.

By sundown, I was exhausted and had been eaten alive by bugs. If a bear had come by, I wouldn't have had any fight left in me. But no bears came even close, although I saw a few of them in the distance. I sat down under a pine tree, looked up at the dying light and wondered if I'd ever make it home again.

Note. From *HIP Reading Assessment*, by L. Jamison (with S.F. Pace, L. Gatzke, & D. Kesslering), 2007, Toronto, ON, Canada: High Interest, p. 68.

FIGURE 8.2. Text Sample for Summary Writing With Teacher Talk Added

Lost in the Woods

I was alive. It was morning ~~and the dawn light had turned everything reddish-orange. When my heart stopped pounding, I realized that~~ I was thirsty and hungry. Even worse, those berries I'd eaten the night before weren't sitting in my stomach too well. ~~That's all I needed—to start throwing up again.~~

It's important that it's morning, but the rest is description—interesting but not important. I don't need to include heart pounding. I can just tell that he is thirsty and hungry and not feeling too well.

~~So I started off, my mouth dry and my stomach heaving.~~ I had a full day of walking ahead of me and there were two people back at the crash site who were depending on me. I was determined to keep on going, ~~no matter how queasy I felt~~.

This is important! I'd say it's the main idea: There are two people at the crash site who need him, so he has to keep walking.

I came across water two hours later. ~~It was only a small stream, but as far as I was concerned, it was the best water I'd ever tasted.~~

Finally, he finds some water to drink.

By afternoon, I was so starved ~~I would have eaten my shoes~~. I decided to risk some of the berries again, despite what they did to my stomach.

By afternoon, he is so hungry that he eats some berries, even though they made him sick last night.

By sundown, I was exhausted and had been eaten alive by bugs. ~~If a bear had come by, I wouldn't have had any fight left in me. But no bears came even close, although I saw a few of them in the distance.~~ I sat down under a pine tree, ~~looked up at the dying light~~ and wondered if I'd ever make it home again.

By sunset, he's exhausted and bitten by bugs. He wonders if he'll ever make it home.

Note. Adapted from *HIP Reading Assessment,* by L. Jamison (with S.F. Pace, L. Gatzke, & D. Kesslering), 2007, Toronto, ON, Canada: High Interest, p. 68.

Although there may be a number of possible ways to summarize the passage in Figure 8.1, here is one example:

In the morning, he was hungry and thirsty, and his stomach wasn't feeling too good. There were two people at the crash site who needed him, so he needed to keep walking all day. He finally found some water to drink, but by afternoon, he was so hungry that he ate some berries, even though they had made him sick the night before. By sunset, he was exhausted and bitten by bugs, and he wondered if he was ever going to make it home again.

Guided Practice: Have students work in pairs or small groups to summarize "Trouble in Grade 5" (see the reproducible at the end of this minilesson). They should use the same process to highlight the main idea and strike through repeated or less important details, then collaboratively write (or present orally) a summary of the text, referring to the main character as "he."

After reading, have the students self-evaluate their summaries by asking themselves the following questions:

- Does my summary include all of the important details?
- Did I leave out details that weren't important?
- Did I combine some details or events that go together?
- Did I put the ideas in my own words?
- Are my details in logical order?
- Did I write in complete sentences?

Independent Application: There are many authentic applications for written summaries in classroom situations. Have students practice independently writing a summary of a literary text or a section from a content area textbook.

Date

Observations

Notes for Future Instruction

Text Sample for Students' Summary Writing

Trouble in Grade 5

Back in grade 5, I was rinsing some paintbrushes in the sink when the fire alarm went off. I told Mrs. P. that I couldn't turn the faucet off, but she ignored me. So, I just lined up with the other kids, and we all marched outside in single file.

That would have been no problem if it had been a fire *alarm*. But it wasn't. It was the real thing.

Some garbage container in the boiler room had gone up in flames. Before long, the fire engines arrived, sirens screaming, and we all watched the firemen go rushing in. In grade 5, that's big excitement!

By the time they came out, it was nearly three o'clock, so the principal dismissed us. I confess: I forgot all about the faucet.

I never did see the actual flood. Some kids say that the water from the coatroom had turned into a tidal wave. Other kids say that water was spurting out the windows and doors of our classroom. I don't know which is true. All I know is that there was water everywhere by the time I got to school. And I was in serious trouble.

Note. From *HIP Reading Assessment*, by L. Jamison (with S.F. Pace, L. Gatzke, & D. Kesslering), 2007, Toronto, ON, Canada: High Interest, p. 68.
From *Marvelous Minilessons for Teaching Intermediate Writing, Grades 4–6* by Lori Jamison Rog. © 2011 International Reading Association. May be copied for classroom use.

Hook, Line, and Sinker

"Hook, line, and sinker" refers to the organizational structure of an open-ended response (see Figure 8.3). The hook is an opening that grabs the reader's attention and makes reference to the prompt, the line is a series of details that make up the body of the piece, and the sinker is the closing, a zinger that wraps the piece up neatly.

This lesson teaches students to use a graphic organizer to plan their responses to test prompts. Limited space encourages efficient and concise planning.

Learning Goal: Students will be able to plan a response with an opening grabber, a coherent middle, and a satisfying conclusion.

Traits: Ideas, organization

FIGURE 8.3. Hook, Line, and Sinker Writing

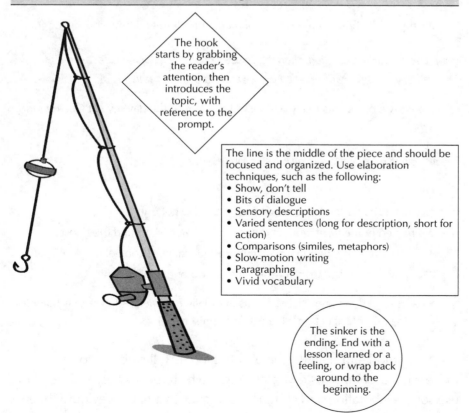

The hook starts by grabbing the reader's attention, then introduces the topic, with reference to the prompt.

The line is the middle of the piece and should be focused and organized. Use elaboration techniques, such as the following:
- Show, don't tell
- Bits of dialogue
- Sensory descriptions
- Varied sentences (long for description, short for action)
- Comparisons (similes, metaphors)
- Slow-motion writing
- Paragraphing
- Vivid vocabulary

The sinker is the ending. End with a lesson learned or a feeling, or wrap back around to the beginning.

NOTES

Date

Observations

Notes for Future Instruction

Introduction: Make a link between good writing and good test writing. Good test writing requires the same elements as good writing: an opening that grabs the reader's attention, a well-developed middle section, and a satisfying ending. Show the fishing pole visual in Figure 8.3.

We all know what good writing looks like. Good test writing is no different than any other type of good writing: It needs a beginning, a middle, and an end. Today, we're going to think about organizing a piece of writing like a fishing pole: The hook is the strong opening that grabs the reader's attention, the line is the middle that is well organized and elaborated, and the sinker is the ending that wraps the piece up neatly.

Instruction: Adapt the Hook, Line, and Sinker Writing reproducible that follows this minilesson to elaboration techniques that you have taught previously. Model for the students how to use the graphic organizer as a quick planner with the following sample or one of your own:

Prompt: Tell about a time when you had a problem and how you solved it.

Grab the reader's attention, then introduce the problem, as requested in the prompt. Try to make reference to the prompt in the first paragraph.

Hook: Are black cats really bad luck? I thought so the day my cat Cookie ran away.

Break down the situation into three or four events.

Line:

1. The babysitter left the door open and Cookie got out.

2. I rushed home from work and frantically searched around the house.

3. I went out in the rain in the neighborhood, calling "Cookie! Cookie!"

4. I came home, and Cookie was lying on top of the television.

Sinker: I still don't know if black cats are really bad luck. All I know is that it's hard to see a black cat on a black television set.

Next, model turning the "line" into a draft. Tell students to try to make each event into its own paragraph, which means they will need to use some elaboration and crafting techniques that have previously been learned in class (see Chapters 4 and 7).

Are black cats really bad luck? I thought so the day my cat Cookie caused a big problem.

    Cookie was an indoor cat. She'd never been outside in her life and never would. That's why I told the new babysitter to be sure not to leave the front door open, so Cookie wouldn't get out. Well, the very first day, I got a panicked phone call "I just left the door open for a minute...." You guessed it. Cookie had disappeared.

    I raced out of my office, leaped into my car, and tore down the road toward home. I dashed frantically through the house from room to room. "Cookie! Cookie!" There was no answer, not even a meow.

    Grabbing an umbrella, I dashed out the front door and down the street in the pouring rain. "Cookie! Cookie!" I cried desperately. I had visions of a scared, drenched cat hiding out under someone's porch.

    Sadly, I returned home, peeled off my wet coat, and sat down on the couch to think about what to do next. "Meow," I heard. I looked up. There was Cookie, draped contentedly on top of the television.

    I still don't know if black cats are really bad luck. All I know is that it's hard to see a black cat on a black television set.

Invite students to identify some of the elaboration and crafting techniques used in this response, such as the magic of three, sentence flipping, vivid verbs, dialogue, and paragraphing.

Guided Practice: Provide students with a prompt such as, "Tell about a problem and how you solved it." Have students complete a hook, line, and sinker organizer. Have them share their planners with a partner and talk through their "lines." Then, each student should draft his or her piece, initially without time constraints. Suggest that students include at least two writing techniques that they have learned, such as those listed in Figure 8.4.

Independent Application: Provide opportunities for students to apply these techniques on their own in untimed and timed situations. Have them highlight special techniques in their writing.

FIGURE 8.4. Writing Techniques Checklist

❑ Showing instead of (or and) telling
❑ Slowing down the action (slow-mo writing)
❑ Bits of dialogue for interest and voice
❑ Sensory descriptions (smells, sounds, tastes, textures, visuals)
❑ Vivid verbs
❑ "Popper" phrases
❑ The magic of three
❑ Comparisons (such as similes)
❑ Varied sentence beginnings
❑ Short, punchy sentences for action or suspense

Date

Observations

Notes for Future Instruction

Hook, Line, and Sinker Writing

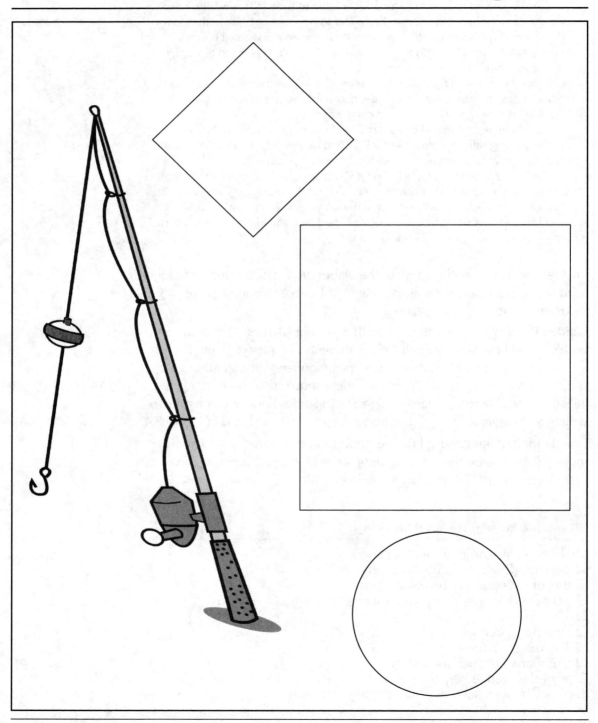

Budgeting Your Time

One of the problems young writers face in test writing is running out of time. Giving students opportunities to practice writing within the limits of the test time will help them get credit on the test for what they know and can do as writers. This lesson is based on a 60-minute time frame, although it could be adapted to any time limit. Needless to say, this will be more than a minilesson if students are to practice working within a testing time frame.

Learning Goal: Students will be able to make optimal use of the time provided to plan, draft, and revise their written responses.

Traits: Ideas, organization, voice, word choice, sentence fluency, conventions

Introduction: Talk to the students about what it means to make a budget.

Usually we think of money when we think of the word <u>budget</u>. We budget our money so that we can plan our spending to make the best use of the money we have—and not spend more money than we have. Budgeting time is the same way. One of the challenges of test writing is that we have a time limit. You have to budget your time so that you can make the best use of the time you have—and not run out of time before you're done. In this lesson, you are going to practice chunking your time for each step of the writing process.

Instruction: Create a visual of a clock (available as a PowerPoint or interactive whiteboard tool) to use as a guide. For the purposes of this minilesson, we will use a 60-minute time frame. Although no process is ever so cut-and-dried, start with this time frame as an example: 15 minutes (one quarter of the time) for planning, 30 minutes (half the time) for drafting, and 15 minutes (the last quarter) for revising and editing. As you practice this timing, make adjustments according to student needs.

Start by providing a prompt or choice of prompts. An Internet search will generate dozens of sites with typical writing prompts for intermediate students, and your department of education is likely to offer released prompts from previous years. The focus here is not the prompt, per se, but the process of responding to it within a time frame.

Tell students that they will have 60 minutes to complete their response, but it will be broken up into planning, drafting, and revising and editing. Start by giving them 15 minutes to plan their responses. Model and discuss some of the things they might do during planning:

Date

Observations

Notes for Future Instruction

NOTES

Date

_____

Observations

_____
_____
_____
_____
_____
_____
_____
_____
_____

Notes for Future Instruction

_____
_____
_____
_____
_____
_____
_____
_____
_____
_____
_____
_____

- *Talk to your brain about what the prompt is asking you to do. Pay attention to whether there is more than one part to the prompt.*

- *Think about what you're going to write. What will you say in response to the prompt? What details might you include?*

- *TAP into voice. Think about your topic, your audience, and your purpose, in other words, who your readers are and what you want them to think or feel about your writing.*

- *Think of how you might open and close the piece. Wow the scorers with a powerful hook and a satisfying wrap-up.*

- *Underline or highlight words or ideas that you will want to use in your response.*

- *Complete a planner or make some notes for yourself.*

Set the timer for 15 minutes. At first, you may want to signal after 10 minutes and again at the "two-minute warning." Tell the students that they may not start drafting until the time is up. (Do a walkabout to monitor, nudge, and encourage.)

When the timer goes off, let the students take a moment's breather, then allow them 30 minutes to draft their writing. Again, before beginning, review key points about the draft:

Remember to double-space your writing, so it looks cleaner and you have room to revise. Always keep your reader in mind and think about your response as a letter to the reader. Write in complete sentences and start a new paragraph when you think you need to. Try to use some of the techniques you've learned for elaboration and writer's craft.

Set the timer for 30 minutes. After 20 minutes, remind students that they have 10 minutes left to complete their drafts. Encourage the students to use as much of the time as possible. If they are done well before 30 minutes, suggest that they add more details. Stop the writing after 30 minutes.

Again, take a break, then allow the last 15 minutes for revision and editing. Your students should have a collection of revision tools in their writing toolboxes, such as carets, strike-throughs, and spider legs. Encourage students to "murmur-read" their writing to ensure that it makes sense and flows logically. Tell them to use the blank lines to insert details or replace mundane words. Refer to the class anchor chart on elaboration and writer's craft strategies to remind students of some of the revisions they may look for.

FIGURE 8.5. A Simple Self-Editing Routine

Use a special editing pen.

Read each sentence twice:

- *First read:* Check the beginning capital and ending punctuation. Read the whole sentence to make sure it makes sense. Add, replace, or take out any words that aren't right.

- *Second read:* Use your pen to tap each word as you read it. Correct the spelling of any words you know. Circle words you're not sure of, so you can look them up later.

Finally, have students take a minute to self-edit the piece. Although conventions count less than we think they do, there is no point in making careless errors. It is also good training for students to make a habit of reviewing their writing before asking someone else to read it. If you haven't taught an editing process, the one in Figure 8.5 works quite effectively. (Note: Occasionally, students will get credit for evidence of editing, even if they haven't made all of the right corrections.)

As you practice timed writing, take note of how students are managing the time. You might want to adjust as you go.

Guided Practice: Continue to practice writing to a timer, gradually releasing responsibility until students are comfortable with the timing and can budget their time.

Independent Application: The independent application will be the test itself. We can only hope that this practice with budgeting time will enable students to make the most of the time frame when they are in an actual testing situation.

NOTES

Date

Observations

Notes for Future Instruction

CHAPTER 9

Supporting Struggling Writers and Beating the Odds

L et's face it, we're all struggling writers. Anyone who claims that writing is easy is either a genius or in denial. George Orwell (1946/1984) once wrote, "Writing a book is a horrible, exhausting struggle, like a long bout of some painful illness" (p. 10). Even Ernest Hemingway is reputed to have said that the scariest thing in the world is a blank piece of paper!

Our students struggle with writing for many different reasons. Many students are dealing with a myriad of circumstances that make learning a challenge, from cognitive to emotional to physical health issues. Strategies for these learners are generally the domain of special interventions. There is evidence that students with learning disabilities make greater gains in the quality of their writing when they are taught to use a process approach and given opportunities to engage in meaningful writing tasks (Marchisan & Alber, 2001).

In these closing pages, I'd like to focus on the "extra scoop" kids—those students who are capable but need another dollop of attention, instruction, or intervention to build both the confidence and the competence that will get them on track as writers.

Building Confidence and Competence

Extra scoop kids experience a range of issues that may lead to writing difficulties: lack of background experience, inadequate vocabulary, struggles with spelling or mechanics. Yet, pretty much all of these students are dealing with a crisis in confidence. After all, writing is a public endeavor. Not only are our thoughts and feelings preserved for posterity but so are our inadequacies with the conventions of writing. As a result, many students simply refuse to try. As Leif Fearn and Nancy Farnan (2008) say, "It isn't so much the struggle that is the problem. Far more problematic is the active avoidance that accompanies a sense of incompetence" (p. 210).

Writers can't become better if they don't write—and they won't write unless they see themselves as capable of success. There is a significant reciprocal relationship between self-concept and academic achievement (Purkey, 1970). As teachers, we have to find ways to help build our students' self-esteem as writers by creating opportunities for success.

The writing workshop offers an ideal opportunity for building confidence and differentiating instruction. Every writer is able to work at his or her own level. The opportunities for choice—of topics, how to organize one's time, and what pieces to take to publication—may be even more empowering to the struggling writer than to some of our star students (who sometimes have learned to succeed by anticipating the teacher's expectations rather than developing their own independent learning skills). The TAG conference and the author's chair (discussed in Chapter 1), in particular, are two routines that enable us to honor the work of all of our writers while stretching each one of them to higher levels.

Providing That Extra Scoop

Struggling writers need the same good teaching that proficient writers need, but they need it even more and often need more of it. Instruction that is guided by analysis of student needs, ongoing assessment, and sensitive scaffolding supports *all* learners, especially those who struggle. Every minilesson in this book is as appropriate for a struggling writer as it is for a strong one. Reluctant writers frequently just need more support along the way.

All young writers need explicit instruction in writing processes, strategies, genres, and techniques. The whole-class minilesson is one way we provide that instruction. We can also use writing time for working with individuals or small groups of students who need an extra scoop of the same strategy, require additional modeling or guided practice, or have particular needs not addressed in the whole group.

Here are 10 tips for teachers to provide additional support for struggling writers:

1. *Allow lots of talk before and during writing.* According to James Collins (1998), struggling writers are more comfortable talking about their ideas than writing them. If students can organize their thinking by pretelling, they can devote more energy to the act of putting those ideas on paper.

2. *Differentiate expectations to meet the needs of the learners.* For example, you may require fewer or shorter pieces of draft or published writing from some students. You might also provide extra conferences, additional editing support, or other detours on the publishing journey.

3. *Encourage independent choice.* Often, our struggling writers respond well to a workshop situation in which they decide what they're going to write and what they're going to publish.

4. *Establish consistent routines for writing workshop, including a regular and predictable schedule.* Include procedures for organizing materials, so students are not wasting writing time looking for a pen or sorting pieces in their writing folders.

5. *Provide opportunities for both "silent" and "quiet" writing time.* For many people, writing is a social activity, but some writers need quiet and freedom from distractions. To allow for both, divide the writing workshop into "silent" writing time and "quiet" writing time. Some teachers play soft music during silent writing time to signal that there is to be no movement or conversation. During "quiet" writing time, students are permitted to move around and talk in quiet voices. Also, cardboard study carrels can be created to minimize distractions for some students.

6. *Don't try to focus on too many things at once, whether in teaching or conferring, revising or editing.* To point out a dozen spelling errors, missing capitalization, and a set of run-on sentences is an invitation for students to ignore all of it. We need to decide what to require and what to let go. If we focus only on one problem at a time, there's a better chance that the writer might actually learn from his or her errors.

7. *Try to provide skills and opportunities for word processing.* According to *Writing Next* (Graham & Perin, 2007), word processing has particular value for struggling writers. Not only does spell-check offer spelling support, the word-processed copy is neater and easier to work with than disastrous handwriting for both the reader and the writer.

8. *Make dictionaries, thesauruses, and other resources available to students for revising and editing.* Take time to teach students how (and how not) to use these materials. Discourage the use of reference materials during drafting; looking up words in the dictionary generally interferes with the flow of the composition.

9. *Chunk time and tasks.* Set small goals, such as five sentences at a time. Allow some students to use timers to time themselves for shorter periods of writing, such as 5 or 10 minutes, then take a break before continuing the writing.

10. *Gradually release responsibility with scaffolding and support.* A framework or sentence scaffold may be a good starting point, but don't allow students to become too dependent on these supports.

The writing workshop provides a structure to meet the needs of a range of students by honoring them wherever they are in their learning, while also encouraging them to extend their reach. For many students, that extra scoop of attention and instruction is all they need to get them on track. But, what about schools where large proportions of students are struggling—and not just in writing?

Beating the Odds Through Writing Instruction

There is a general consensus that low socioeconomic schools produce low academic achievement (Chall, Jacobs, & Baldwin, 1990). But writing instruction may very well be a key to beating the odds! In his research on "90/90/90 schools," Douglas Reeves (2005, p. 185) analyzed schools with 90% students living in poverty, 90% belonging to ethnic minorities, *and* 90% scoring at or above standard on independent assessments. What is these schools' secret to success? That's what Reeves sought to find out. He learned that they had some very specific elements in common: None relied on a particular literacy program, and all put an emphasis on writing.

In the most successful schools in Reeves's study, writing played an important role in virtually every subject area and almost every assessment. Writing was found to help students organize and clarify their thinking and provided teachers with richer diagnostic information than simply right or wrong answers on tests. In addition, in these schools, teachers used professional time to collaborate on both planning and assessment. In fact, collaborative assessment was a key feature of the successful schools. When teachers sit down to score student writing together, they benefit not only from more consistent and fair grading practices but also by building a common language and understanding of the qualities of good writing.

Recognizing that they couldn't focus on everything at once, the teachers at the 90/90/90 schools chose to put their energies into reading, writing, and mathematics. Writing, especially nonfiction, was integrated into every subject area. The teachers quickly learned that most students couldn't write up experiments in science or write literary essays in language arts unless they were taught the structures and expectations of those types of writing. Ultimately, every teacher became a teacher of writing.

This is not radical thinking. Over 100 years ago, the National Educational Association's (1894) Committee of Ten on Secondary School Studies wrote, "The study of every other subject should contribute to the pupil's training in English; and that the pupil's capacity to write English should be made available, and be developed, in every other department" (p. 21). When the 90/90/90 schools focused on literacy and numeracy, their students grew in other areas as well. As Reeves (2005) reports, "It is difficult to escape the conclusion that an emphasis on writing improvement has a significant impact on student test scores in other disciplines, including science" (p. 190).

In his work on 21st-century skills, Tony Wagner (2008) includes written communication as one of the seven essential skills for success. According to Wagner, concerns about writing are not so much about grammar or conventions; they are more about fuzzy thinking and lack of voice: Writers in all walks of professional life must learn to be clear and concise, while at the same time, focused, energetic, and passionate about the points they want to make. If we want our students to be able to articulate their thinking in writing, we must provide them with the tools for crafting their ideas in writing. That's what the minilessons in this book are about.

Not every student of writing will become a published author, not every music student will perform at the Metropolitan Opera, and not every junior hockey player will win the Stanley Cup. This doesn't mean we should give up on them. Instead, we should be inspired to do what we can to encourage every student to write the very best they can, to sing the very best they can, to be the very best they can. In education, our job is not to create superstars but to encourage the everyday stars in our classrooms to shine a little brighter each day.

I often say that writing a book is a bit like giving birth—but it takes longer and is more painful. Fortunately, there are many people who help along the way.

Thank you to my friend and colleague, Adrienne Gear (2006), for permission to use the BIBB (Bring It Back to the Book) strategy (see Chapter 8) described in her terrific reading comprehension book *Reading Power: Teaching Students to Think While They Read.*

Thank you to Steve Peha, of Teaching That Makes Sense, for permission to adapt the "What-Why-How" planner in Chapter 6. Check out ttms.org for this and many more great ideas for writing.

Thank you to many colleagues across North America who invited me into their classrooms and districts to talk about writing and learn together. In particular, thanks to Principal Pam Davis-Webb and her literacy support team, Christine Thomas and Suzanne Comstock, and the rest of the faculty at Diven Elementary School in Elmira, New York, whose work on units of study is shared in Chapter 2.

Thank you to my editors, Stacey Reid and Susanne Viscarra, who kept my research ducks in a row and my citations in place; to Shannon Fortner for her patience in working with me to put the book together; and to IRA for another fine job of producing a book both friendly and professional.

Thank you to those schools and districts that are recognizing the importance of writing in the literacy development of today's students—and making it an important part of the curricula.

Most important, thank you to my husband and favorite author, Paul Kropp, who's my cheerleader, who keeps me disciplined when I can find a hundred other things to do instead of writing, and who has allowed me to doctor several excerpts of his young adult novels to create guided writing activities for this book.

Allen, P.A. (2009). *Conferring: The keystone of reader's workshop.* Portland, ME: Stenhouse.

Anderson, J. (2007). *Everyday editing: Inviting students to develop skill and craft in writer's workshop.* Portland, ME: Stenhouse.

Angelillo, J. (2005). *Writing to the prompt: When students don't have a choice.* Portsmouth, NH: Heinemann.

Atwell, N. (1998). *In the middle: New understandings about writing, reading, and learning* (2nd ed.). Portsmouth, NH: Boynton/Cook.

Bamberg, B. (2003). Revision. In I.L. Clark (with B. Bamberg, D. Bowden, J.R. Edlund, L. Gerrard, S. Klein, et al.), *Concepts in composition: Theory and practice in the teaching of writing* (pp. 107–140). Mahwah, NJ: Erlbaum.

Barrs, M., & Pidgeon, S. (1994). *Reading the difference: Gender and reading in elementary classrooms.* York, ME: Stenhouse.

Bausell, C.V. (2008). Tracking U.S. trends: States vary in classroom access to computers and in policies concerning school technology. *Education Week, 27*(30), 39–42.

Benton, S.L., & Blohm, P.J. (1988). Elaboration of ideas in prose production. *Journal of Experimental Education, 56*(2), 60–66.

Braddock, R. (1975). The frequency and placement of topic sentences in expository prose. *Research in the Teaching of English, 8*(3), 287–302.

Buzan, T. (with Buzan, B.). (1993). *The mind map book: How to use radiant thinking to maximize your brain's untapped potential.* New York: Plume.

Calkins, L.M. (1983). *Lessons from a child: On the teaching and learning of writing.* Exeter, NH: Heinemann.

Calkins, L.M. (1986). *The art of teaching writing.* Portsmouth, NH: Heinemann.

Calkins, L., Montgomery, K., & Santman, D. (with Falk, B.). (1998). *A teacher's guide to standardized reading tests: Knowledge is power.* Portsmouth, NH: Heinemann.

Chall, J.S., Jacobs, V.A., & Baldwin, L.E. (1990). *The reading crisis: Why poor children fall behind.* Cambridge, MA: Harvard University Press.

Chevalier, T. (n.d.). *Girl with a pearl earring: Inspiration.* Retrieved July 26, 2010, from www.tchevalier.com/gwape/inspiration/index.html

Christensen, F., & Christensen, B. (1978). *Notes toward a new rhetoric: Nine essays for teachers* (2nd ed.). New York: Harper & Row.

Collins, J.L. (1998). *Strategies for struggling writers.* New York: Guilford.

Conzemius, A., & O'Neill, J. (with Commodore, C.). (2006). *The power of SMART goals: Using goals to improve student learning.* Bloomington, IN: Solution Tree.

Cooper, F.T. (1920). *The craftsmanship of writing.* New York: Dodd, Mead. (Original work published 1910)

Cowan, G., & Cowan, E. (1980). *Writing.* New York: Wiley.

Crowhurst, M. (1990). Teaching and learning the writing of persuasive/argumentative discourse. *Canadian Journal of Education, 15*(4), 348–359.

Culham, R. (2003). *6+1 traits of writing: The complete guide, grades 3 and up.* New York: Scholastic.

Cunningham, P.M., Cunningham, J.W., Hall, D.P., & Moore, S.A. (2005). *Writing the four-blocks way.* Greensboro, NC: Carson-Dellosa.

Diederich, P.B. (1974). *Measuring growth in English.* Urbana, IL: National Council of Teachers of English.

Durst, R.K. (1984). The development of analytic writing. In A.N. Applebee (Ed.), *Contexts for learning to write: Studies of secondary school instruction* (pp. 79–102). Norwood, NJ: Ablex.

Elbow, P. (1973). *Writing without teachers.* New York: Oxford University Press.

Elbow, P., & Belanoff, P. (2000). *Sharing and responding* (3rd ed.). New York: McGraw-Hill.

Engel, S.M. (2000). *With good reason: An introduction to informal fallacies* (6th ed.). Boston: Bedford/St. Martin's.

Fearn, L., & Farnan, N. (2008). Classroom instruction for struggling writers. In S. Lenski & J. Lewis (Eds.), *Reading success for struggling adolescent learners* (pp. 209–226). New York: Guilford.

Fletcher, R., & Portalupi, J. (2001). *Writing workshop: The essential guide.* Portsmouth, NH: Heinemann.

Gallick-Jackson, S.A. (1997). *Improving narrative writing skills, composition skills, and related attitudes among second grade students by integrating word processing, graphic organizers, and art into a process approach to writing.* Unpublished practicum report, Nova Southeastern University, Fort Lauderdale-Davie, FL. (ERIC Document Reproduction Service No. ED420064)

Gardner, H. (2004). *Frames of mind: The theory of multiple intelligences* (20th anniversary ed.). New York: Basic.

Gear, A. (2006). *Reading power: Teaching students to think while they read.* Markham, ON, Canada: Pembroke.

Gere, A.R. (1987). *Writing groups: History, theory, and implications.* Carbondale: Southern Illinois University Press.

Graham, S., & Perin, D. (2007). *Writing next: Effective strategies to improve writing of adolescents in middle and high schools—A report to Carnegie Corporation of New York.* New York: Alliance for Excellent Education.

Graves, D.H. (1983). *Writing: Teachers and children at work.* Exeter, NH: Heinemann.

Graves, D.H. (1994). *A fresh look at writing.* Portsmouth, NH: Heinemann.

Graves, D. (n.d.). Answering your questions about teaching writing: A talk with Donald H. Graves. *Instructor.* Retrieved July 20, 2010, from www2.scholastic.com/browse/article.jsp?id=4415

Graves, D., & Hansen, J. (1983). The author's chair. *Language Arts, 60*(2), 176–183.

Hansen, J. (1987). *When writers read.* Portsmouth, NH: Heinemann.

Harvey, S., & Goudvis, A. (2007). *Strategies that work: Teaching comprehension for understanding and engagement* (2nd ed.). Portland, ME: Stenhouse; Markham, ON, Canada: Pembroke.

Hendrickson, L. (1980). Procedures and results of an evaluation of writing. *Educational Evaluation and Policy Analysis, 2*(4), 19–30.

Hillocks, G., Jr. (1986). *Research on written composition: New directions for teaching.* Urbana, IL: ERIC Clearinghouse on Reading and Communication Skills & National Conference on Research in English.

Huot, B. (1990). The literature of direct writing assessment: Major concerns and prevailing trends. *Review of Educational Research, 60*(2), 237–263.

Jacobs, G. (1986). Quickwriting: A technique for invention in writing. *ELT Journal, 40*(4), 282–290. doi:10.1093/elt/40.4.282

Jacobson, J. (2010). *No more "I'm done!" Fostering independent writers in the primary grades.* Portland, ME: Stenhouse.

Jamison, L (with Pace, S.F., Gatzke, L., & Kesslering, D.). (2007). *HIP reading assessment.* Toronto, ON, Canada: High Interest.

King, S. (2000). *On writing: A memoir of the craft.* New York: Pocket.

Kissner, E. (2006). *Summarizing, paraphrasing and retelling: Skills for better reading, writing, and test taking.* Portsmouth, NH: Heinemann.

Kress, G. (2003). *Literacy in the new media age*. New York: Routledge.

Kroll, B.M. (1984). Audience adaptation in children's persuasive letters. *Written Communication, 1*(4), 407–427. doi:10.1177/0741088384001004002

Lane, B. (1993). *After the end: Teaching and learning creative revision*. Portsmouth, NH: Heinemann.

Lane, B., & Bernabei, G. (2001). *Why we must run with scissors: Voice lessons in persuasive writing 3–12*. Shoreham, VT: Discover Writing.

Langer, J.A. (2002). *Effective literacy instruction: Building successful reading and writing programs*. Urbana, IL: National Council of Teachers of English.

Lorcher, T. (2010, February 22). *Improving writing by improving word choice* [Blog]. Retrieved August 5, 2010, from www.brighthub.com/education/homework-tips/articles/33495.aspx

MacArthur, C.A. (1996). Using technology to enhance the writing processes of students with learning disabilities. *Journal of Learning Disabilities, 29*(4), 344–354. doi:10.1177/002221949602900403

Marchisan, M.L., & Alber, S.R. (2001). The write way: Tips for teaching the writing process to resistant writers. *Intervention in School and Clinic, 36*(3), 154–162.

Marzano, R.J., Norford, J.S., Paynter, D.E., Pickering, D.J., & Gaddy, B.B. (2001). *A handbook for classroom instruction that works*. Alexandria, VA: Association for Supervision and Curriculum Development.

Millard, E. (1997). Differently literate: Gender identity and the construction of the developing reader. *Gender and Education, 9*(1), 31–48. doi:10.1080/09540259721439

Moore, K.D. (2009). *Effective instructional strategies: From theory to practice* (2nd ed.). Thousand Oaks, CA: Sage.

The National Commission on Writing in America's Schools and Colleges. (2003). *The neglected "R": The need for a writing revolution*. New York: College Entrance Examination Board.

National Educational Association. (1894). *Report of the Committee of Ten on Secondary School Studies*. New York: American Book.

Newkirk, T. (2009). *Holding on to good ideas in a time of bad ones: Six literacy principles worth fighting for*. Portsmouth, NH: Heinemann.

Obama, B.H. (2009, January 21). *President Barack Obama's inaugural address*. Retrieved August 5, 2010, from www.whitehouse.gov/blog/inaugural-address/

Ontario Ministry of Education. (2008). *A guide to effective literacy instruction, grades 4 to 6. Volume 6: Writing*. Toronto, ON, Canada: Queen's Printer for Ontario.

Orwell, G. (1984). Why I write. In *Why I write* (pp. 1–10). New York: Penguin. (Reprinted from *Gangrel*, Summer 1946, pp. 5–10)

Palincsar, A.S., & Brown, A.L. (1986). Interactive teaching to promote independent learning from text. *The Reading Teacher, 39*(8), 771–777.

Pearson, P.D., & Gallagher, M.C. (1983). The instruction of reading comprehension. *Contemporary Educational Psychology, 8*(3), 317–344. doi:10.1016/0361-476X(83)90019-X

Peha, S. (1995). The writing strategy organizer. In *The organizers* (p. 3). Carrboro, NC: Teaching That Makes Sense. Retrieved August 4, 2010, from ttms.org/PDFs/15%20Organizers%20v001%20(Full).pdf

Piaget, J. (1952). *The origins of intelligence in children* (M. Cook, Trans.). New York: International Universities Press.

Purkey, W.W. (1970). *Self concept and school achievement*. Englewood Cliffs, NJ: Prentice Hall.

Reeves, D.B. (2005). *Accountability in action: A blueprint for learning organizations* (2nd ed.). Englewood, CO: Advanced Learning.

Rickey, J. (2010). *The better answer game* [Interactive student game]. Retrieved August 9, 2010, from www.netrover.com/~kingskid/Better_Answer/answer.html

Rief, L. (2003). *100 quickwrites: Fast and effective freewriting exercises that build students' confidence, develop their fluency, and bring out the writer in every student.* New York: Scholastic.

Rog, L.J. (1996). *Love of writing handbook.* Regina, SK, Canada: Regina Public Schools.

Rog, L.J. (2007). *Marvelous minilessons for teaching beginning writing, K–3.* Newark, DE: International Reading Association.

Rog, L.J., & Kropp, P. (2004). *The write genre: Classroom activities and mini-lessons that promote writing with clarity, style and flashes of brilliance.* Markham, ON, Canada: Pembroke.

Ronis, D.L. (2008). *Clustering standards in integrated units* (2nd ed.). Thousand Oaks, CA: Corwin.

Roser, N.L., & Bomer, K. (2005). Writing in primary classrooms: A teacher's story. In R. Indrisano & J.R. Paratore (Eds.), *Learning to write, writing to learn: Theory and research in practice* (pp. 26–39). Newark, DE: International Reading Association.

Routman, R. (2005). *Writing essentials: Raising expectations and results while simplifying teaching.* Portsmouth, NH: Heinemann.

Santa, C.M. (with Havens, L., Nelson, M., Danner, M., Scalf, L., & Scalf, J.). (1988). *Content reading including study systems: Reading, writing and studying across the curriculum.* Dubuque, IA: Kendall/Hunt.

Smith, C.G. (2008). Braddock revisited: The frequency and placement of topic sentences in academic writing. *The Reading Matrix, 8*(1), 78–95.

Snyder, I. (Ed.). (1998). *Page to screen: Taking literacy into the electronic era.* New York: Routledge.

Spandel, V. (2001). *Creating writers through 6-trait writing assessment and instruction* (3rd ed.). New York: Addison Wesley Longman.

Stiggins, R.J. (1988). Revitalizing classroom assessment: The highest instructional priority. *Phi Delta Kappan, 69*(5), 363–368.

Stronge, J.H. (2007). *Qualities of effective teachers* (2nd ed.). Alexandria, VA: Association for Supervision and Curriculum Development.

Tompkins, G.E. (2000). *Teaching writing: Balancing process and product* (3rd ed.). Upper Saddle River, NJ: Merrill.

Tyler, R.W. (1969). Basic principles of curriculum and instruction. Chicago: University of Chicago Press. (Original work published 1949)

Volante, L. (2004). Teaching to the test: What every educator and policy-maker should know. *Canadian Journal of Educational Administration and Policy, 35*. Retrieved September 2, 2010, from www.umanitoba.ca/publications/cjeap/articles/volante.html

Wagner, T. (2008). Rigor redefined. *Educational Leadership, 66*(2), 20–25.

Wiggins, G., & McTighe, J. (1998). *Understanding by design* (2nd ed.). Alexandria, VA: Association for Supervision and Curriculum Development.

Wilkinson, A., Barnsley, G., Hanna, P., & Swan, M. (1980). *Assessing language development.* Oxford, England: Oxford University Press.

Writing Study Group of the NCTE Executive Committee. (2004). NCTE beliefs about the teaching of writing. Urbana, IL: National Council of Teachers of English. Retrieved April 15, 2010, from www.ncte.org/positions/statements/writingbeliefs?source=gs

Yancey, K.B. (2009). *Writing in the 21st century.* Urbana, IL: National Council of Teachers of English. Available: www.ncte.org/library/NCTEFiles/Press/Yancey_final.pdf

Yinger, R.J. (1980). A study of teacher planning. *The Elementary School Journal, 80*(3), 107–127.

Children's Literature Cited

Avi. (2004). *The end of the beginning: Being the adventures of a small snail (and an even smaller ant)*. Orlando, FL: Harcourt.

Cleary, B. (2000). *The mouse and the motorcycle*. New York: HarperTrophy. (Original work published 1965)

Collard, S.B., III. (1997). *Animal dads*. Boston: Houghton Mifflin.

Collard, S.B., III. (2002). *Beaks!* Watertown, MA: Charlesbridge.

Collard, S.B., III. (2008). *Teeth*. Watertown, MA: Charlesbridge.

Dahl, R. (1988). *Matilda*. New York: Viking.

Fletcher, R. (1997). *Twilight comes twice*. New York: Clarion.

Frame, J.A. (2003). *Yesterday I had the blues*. Berkeley, CA: Tricycle.

Juster, N. (1989). *As: A surfeit of similes*. New York: Morrow.

Kropp, P. (2002). *The countess and me*. Markham, ON, Canada: Fitzhenry & Whiteside.

Kropp, P. (2003). *Ghost house*. Toronto, ON, Canada: High Interest.

Kropp, P. (2005). *The crash*. Toronto, ON, Canada: High Interest.

Kropp, P. (2006). *Shooting the rapids*. Toronto, ON, Canada: High Interest.

Kropp, P. (2008). *Winner!* Toronto, ON, Canada: High Interest.

Layne, S.L. (2003). *My brother Dan's delicious*. Gretna, LA: Pelican.

O'Neill, M. (2009). *Hailstones and halibut bones: Adventures in color*. New York: Delacorte. (Original work published 1961)

Orloff, K.K. (2004). *I wanna iguana*. New York: New York: G.P. Putnam's Sons.

Simon, S. (2008). *The human body*. Washington, DC: Smithsonian Institution; New York: Collins.

Smith, R. (2009, December 16). A real-life Superman. *Time for Kids*. Retrieved August 3, 2010, from www.timeforkids.com/TFK/kids/news/story/0,28277,1948139,00.html

Teague, M. (2002). *Dear Mrs. LaRue: Letters from obedience school*. New York: Scholastic.

Timberlake, A. (2003). *The dirty cowboy*. New York: Farrar Straus Giroux.

Wisniewski, D. (1998). *The secret knowledge of grown-ups*. New York: Lothrop, Lee & Shepard.

Note. Page numbers followed by *f*, *t*, or *r* indicate figures, tables, or reproducibles, respectively.